Polymer Clay
for the *Fun* of it!

Kim Cavender

NORTH LIGHT BOOKS
CINCINNATI, OHIO
www.artistsnetwork.com

Distributed in Canada by Fraser Direct
100 Armstrong Avenue
Georgetown, ON, Canada L7G 5S4

Distributed in the U.K. and Europe by David & Charles
Brunel House, Newton Abbot, Devon, TQ12 4PU, England
Tel: (+44) 1626 323200, Fax: (+44) 1626 323319
Email: mail@davidandcharles.co.uk

Distributed in Australia by Capricorn Link
P.O. Box 704, Windsor, NSW 2756 Australia

10   09   08   07   06   5   4   3   2   1

Library of Congress Cataloging-in-Publication Data

Cavender, Kim
    Polymer clay for the fun of it / Kim Cavender.-- 1st ed.
       p. cm.
    Includes index.
    ISBN 1-58180-684-1 (alk. paper)
    1. Polymer clay craft. I. Title.
    TT297.C44 2005
    745.57'2--dc22
                                    2005011035

Editor: JESSICA GORDON

Cover Designer: MARISSA BOWERS

Interior Designer: LEIGH ANN LENTZ

Layout Artist: KATHY BERGSTROM

Production Coordinator: MATT WAGNER

Photographers: CHRISTINE POLOMSKY
                        HAL BARKAN
                        TIM GRONDIN

Stylist: JAN NICKUM

metric conversion chart

To convert	to	multiply by
Inches	Centimeters	2.54
Centimeters	Inches	0.4
Feet	Centimeters	30.5
Centimeters	Feet	0.03
Yards	Meters	0.9
Meters	Yards	1.1
Sq. Inches	Sq. Centimeters	6.45
Sq. Centimeters	Sq. Inches	0.16
Sq. Feet	Sq. Meters	0.09
Sq. Meters	Sq. Feet	10.8
Sq. Yards	Sq. Meters	0.8
Sq. Meters	Sq. Yards	1.2
Pounds	Kilograms	0.45
Kilograms	Pounds	2.2
Ounces	Grams	28.3
Grams	Ounces	0.035

DEDICATION

I dedicate this book to my husband and children for all the patience, help, advice and encouragement they gave me during the wonderfully exciting, sometimes frustrating, but always enjoyable creative journey I embarked on while writing this book. And to my parents, for always being there in every way. My love and gratitude to you all.

ABOUT THE AUTHOR

After experimenting with many different mediums, artist and designer Kim Cavender has been working exclusively with polymer clay for over six years. She travels frequently to teach and demonstrate the exciting medium of polymer clay at workshops and trade shows across the country.

She has appeared on HGTV's *The Carol Duvall Show* and has been published in various magazines, including *Expression* and *Polymer Café*. Her work has been featured in the books *Faux Surfaces in Polymer Clay*, *400 Polymer Creations* and *Elegant Gifts in Polymer Clay*.

She started her own business, It's Out of My Hands, several years ago as interest in her artwork began to grow. In addition to selling her pieces through her company, Kim is a juried artisan at Tamarack: The Best of West Virginia, and her work has been exhibited at shows across the country as well. She is a founding member of the Kanawha Valley Polymer Clay Guild, a member of the National Polymer Clay Guild and the polymer clay guilds in both Columbus, Ohio and Pittsburgh, Pennsylvania.

She holds a B.A. degree in English and Journalism from Marshall University. Kim lives in West Virginia with her husband Ben, her sons Daniel and Adam, and a neurotic schnauzer named Buster. Contact Kim through her website, www.kimcavender.com.

ACKNOWLEDGMENTS

First, I would like to thank the many polymer clay artists and teachers who have shared their talent and expertise so generously through articles, books and classes.

A big thank you to Carol Duvall, a truly gracious lady, for helping to bring the amazing medium of polymer clay into homes all over the world (including mine) and for allowing me the privilege of standing next to the "Queen of Crafts."

To my friend and mentor, Donna Kato, who has been so generous and kind in affording me the opportunity to do what I love, thanks for 1001 things, but especially for creating the ultimate polymer clay and sharing your talent with us all.

To my fellow Kato-etts: Judy Belcher, Leslie Blackford, Cathy Johnston, Sue Kelsey, KLEW, Jacqueline Lee and Gail Ritchey. Your friendship, humor and encouragement are worth their weight in diamond tiaras and other assorted headgear. To Lisa Pavelka, my cosmic robe twin, bathroom buddy, and cheerleader extraordinaire, thanks for your encouragement, advice and friendship.

To fly girl Debbie Jackson and her beautiful book, *Polymer Clay Jewelry*, thanks for reinforcing my belief in serendipity and for being my saving grace on a Wednesday in November.

To my fellow members of the Kanawha Valley and Pittsburgh Polymer Clay Guilds, thanks for making our clay days and retreats so special.

A big thank you to Robert Augur, Tony Aquino and the team at Van Aken for your vision, support and encouragement and for supplying all the clay used in the book.

My gratitude to all the wonderful companies who supplied me with the materials and products used in the book. I can honestly say that each and every product I used was a joy to work with. Your support and generosity made my job a whole lot easier and a lot more fun.

Last, but certainly not least, I couldn't ask for a more wonderful group of people to work with than those at F+W Publications. To my "fresh and easy" pal Greg Hatfield, thanks for picking me out of the crowd. My appreciation to Christine Doyle, who didn't let me weasel out of that book proposal and answered way too many questions with the patience of a saint. To Tricia Waddell, thanks for your encouragement and faith in me. And finally, the ultimate dream team! Thank you to my editor, Jessica Gordon, who kept me focused (not an easy task!) and never lost her cool or her ability to help me keep mine. Another big thank you goes to my brilliant photographer, Christine Polomsky, who kept me laughing when I should have been crying. Baaa! That's sheep talk for thank you. Next time, guys, lunch at Panera Bread is on me! Thank you also to Leigh Ann Lentz for her beautifully playful book design.

WHAT'S INSIDE

JEWELRY AND ACCESSORIES 20

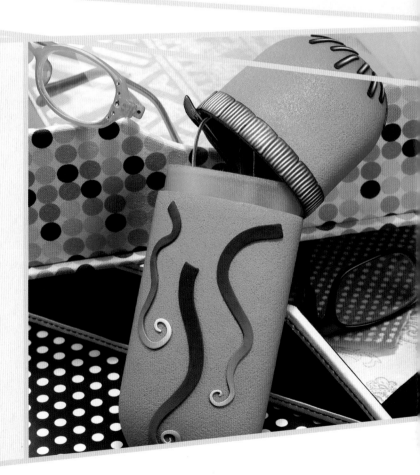

OFFICE ESSENTIALS 62

EXTRAORDINARY HOME DÉCOR 88

INTRODUCTION

For as long as I can remember, I've felt the desire to create. I went to college believing I would be a writer, but after earning my degree I realized my hands needed to do more than just put words on paper. The need to create never left me, and I spent several years working with almost every art material available. I became frustrated with the limits of each one, and kept looking for the medium that fit me best. Then, one day I picked up polymer clay and discovered an art material with no limits at all.

If you've worked with polymer clay before, you already know how magical it is. If you haven't, I hope this book will help get you started on your own creative journey with this amazing medium.

I've developed some unique and exciting projects that will expose you to a wide variety of the techniques and effects that are possible with polymer clay. More than anything else, I hope you have fun and laugh along the way. Try not to agonize over the details—just learn the techniques and enjoy the creative process.

In the following pages, you'll find basic information and step-by-step techniques designed for both beginners and those who have experience working with polymer clay. In addition, you'll find fun, original projects including jewelry, personal accessories, and office and home décor items. The projects are arranged within each section beginning with those that are less complex. Many of the projects also include a special "Just for the fun of it …" feature I know you'll enjoy. In addition, you'll find an inspirational gallery section (see pages 120-123) with some fabulous eye candy and a resource guide (see pages 124-125) to help you locate any of the products you may need to complete the projects.

Writing this book has been an amazing experience for me and a dream come true. I feel very fortunate to be doing something I love so much, and I continue to learn something new about the clay—and often about myself—each time I pick it up.

I hope you learn a few things as you work with polymer clay as well. Put on some inspiring music and sit down with a few blocks of clay—you'll find that it's pure rejuvenation, like taking a little soul vacation. Picasso (who would've kicked butt with polymer clay) said, "Art washes away from the soul the dust of everyday life." There are few things in life as true.

"If you never did, you should. These things are fun, and fun is good."
—Dr. Seuss

POLYMER CLAY PRIMER

Polymer clay is definitely the most fun, exciting and versatile material in the world of arts and crafts today. What other art material can you sculpt, mold, texture, carve, paint, sand, drill, stamp, fold, stack, roll, stretch and even sew? Polymer clay also comes in a liquid form, which adds even greater variety. Although it's referred to as a clay, it's actually a synthetic material composed of polyvinyl chloride (PVC), colored pigment, plasticizer and a bit of pure magic. It's a relatively new material as far as art mediums are concerned, and artists are just beginning to explore its possibilities. By following some basic guidelines and familiarizing yourself with a few techniques, you'll see how easy and fun it can be to create beautiful pieces of your own. Trust me, it's not rocket science!

WHAT CLAY SHOULD I CHOOSE?

All of the projects in this book were created with Kato Polyclay. However, there are several brands of clay available, each with different characteristics. All of the clays listed below are also available in liquid form.

Kato Polyclay is both extremely strong and flexible when baked. It's easy to condition and its color doesn't change or darken regardless of how many times it's baked. One of its best features is that it never feels sticky or too soft, even after being worked for long periods of time. For this reason, it's a great choice for those who like to make *millefiori* canes and don't have the patience or time to let them sit overnight before cutting them. It comes in a variety of colors, including metallics and translucent, and is available in both small and large packages.

Fimo Classic is more difficult to condition than Kato but is also great for caning. It holds detail well and is very strong after baking, but without much flexibility. It also comes in a large variety of colors and is available in both small and large packages.

Fimo Soft is easier to condition than the classic variety, but it is not as strong and durable after baking.

Premo! Sculpey is easy to condition and is also strong and flexible after baking. It comes in a large selection of colors including metallics and translucent. It has a tendency to become quite soft after repeated manipulation. Canes made with Premo may need to rest for a day or two so they can be sliced without distortion.

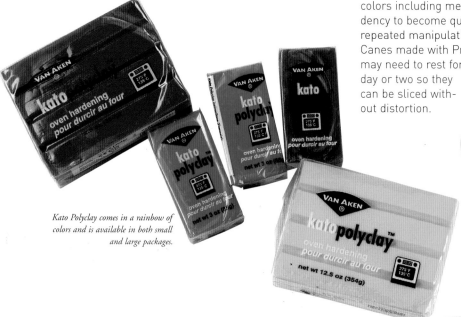

Kato Polyclay comes in a rainbow of colors and is available in both small and large packages.

PSST... HERE'S A TIP

If the clay you're using is too soft and sticky, you may need to leach out some of the plasticizers by placing the clay between layers of parchment paper or brown grocery bags and letting it sit on your work surface for a few hours or overnight.

CONDITIONING POLYMER CLAY

All types of clay must be conditioned to ensure that the plasticizers and PVC particles are evenly dispersed. A pasta machine is most often used to condition polymer clay. If you spend any amount of time working with polymer clay, a pasta machine is invaluable and well worth the investment, especially for conditioning. To begin conditioning clay, cut slices of clay a little thicker than the largest setting on your pasta machine and begin running them through the machine until the clay has a uniform feel and consistency. You can also condition clay by kneading and twisting it.

CHOOSING A WORK SURFACE

Of all of the different work surfaces I've tried, Formica is my favorite. You can also work on a ceramic tile, a thick sheet of glass, a marble slab and some types of plastic. Large ceramic tiles can be purchased inexpensively from your local home improvement store, and if you're lucky enough to know a builder or someone who's remodeling a kitchen, you may be able to acquire my favorite work surface, the "sink hole." When workers install Formica countertops in a kitchen, they cut out a hole for the sink and discard the cut-out section of Formica. By attaching a handle along one edge of the section, you have a great transportable work surface. Never place uncured polymer clay on a wooden surface as the plasticizers will damage the finish.

STORING POLYMER CLAY

Polymer clay should be stored away from heat and light. High temperatures can actually begin to cook the clay, making it unusable. However, if properly stored, polymer clay has a shelf life of several years. Canes can be stored in plastic containers or wrapped in Saran Wrap (some other brands of plastic wrap are not compatible with polymer clay). Plastic zip-top bags are also a convenient way to store clay. It's a good idea to place a small piece of uncured clay in a potential storage container for a few days to make sure that the plastic used in the container and the plasticizers in the clay are compatible. Incompatible plastics can sometimes fuse together because of a chemical reaction.

BAKING POLYMER CLAY

As a general rule, bake polymer clay at 275°F (175°C) for 15–20 minutes for every ¼" (6mm) of thickness. However, you should always read the instructions because baking times and temperatures may vary depending on the brand of clay. When in doubt, read the instructions! It's also a good idea to use an oven thermometer to make sure that your oven's thermostat is accurate.

Polymer clay can be safely cured in a home oven, a convection oven or a toaster oven. Never bake polymer clay in a microwave, and never bake food and polymer clay in the same oven at the same time. If you plan on working with polymer clay regularly, you may want to purchase a portable oven specifically for baking it. Check garage or tag sales or online auctions for used ovens that you can use to bake clay.

If you notice smoke or a strong odor coming from your oven, immediately turn off the oven and take out the clay. Open the windows to air out the room and remove all pets and people until the fumes and smoke have cleared. Polymer clay or any plastic can emit toxic fumes while burning.

Baking surfaces for polymer clay vary. I bake clay on index cards, ceramic tiles or in a pan lined with baking parchment. If polymer clay is baked directly on glass or ceramic tile, the side facing down will be shiny.

TOOLS

It doesn't take a large investment to acquire the basic tools and equipment you'll need to begin working with polymer clay. A pasta machine, a clay blade, a work surface and, of course, a few blocks of clay will get you started.

However, I do feel obligated to warn you that these items are just the beginning. It won't be long until you begin looking at every kitchen and household gadget as a possible polymer clay tool. Every texture you see will scream to be impressed into clay. Every moldable button and bauble will call your name. And anything that sits still for any length of time becomes a potential target for covering with clay.

Of course, there are also several companies producing tools and materials specifically for use with polymer clay, and the crossover potential with scrapbooking, rubber stamping, beading and other areas of the craft world continues to feed the addiction of polymer junkies. I've listed the tools you'll need to complete the projects in this book and some additional items you may find helpful.

ROLLING TOOLS

A **pasta machine** is the best investment you can make if you're serious about working with polymer clay. It makes conditioning clay much easier and enables you to roll sheets of uniform thickness. There are several brands of pasta machines and each has an adjustable dial that allows you to vary the thickness of the sheets. I used an Atlas machine for the projects in this book. My machine has nine different settings, with the no. 1 setting being the thickest at 1/8" (3mm). Remember that you may need to adjust the project instructions if you're using a different brand of pasta machine.

An **acrylic roller** or **brayer** is another essential tool. They're useful for adhering sheets of clay together and for helping to reduce square canes. I also use large knitting needles as rolling tools to ensure that transfers make good contact with the clay and to smooth cane slices into sheets of clay.

Clockwise from left: plastic texture sheet (bottom), sun face mold, small circle mold, rubber texture sheet (bottom), angled clay lift, clay shaper, needle tool and large knitting needle

SHAPING AND FORMING TOOLS

There's a multitude of tools to help you shape and form polymer clay in both baked and unbaked forms, from gadgets that poke holes and create circular impressions to those that act as structural aids. Get creative when you need a tool—look around for everyday household items that can be adapted for polymer clay use.

Needle tools are great for piercing holes in unbaked beads, and they can also be used to impress lines and add texture to clay. A **bamboo skewer** can also be used to drill holes in unbaked clay.

A **ball stylus** comes in different sizes and can be used on unbaked clay to create a circular impression.

Clay lift tools are great for smoothing the edges of unbaked clay and for scooping out small amounts of mica powder onto clay or onto your work surface. They come in both straight and angled varieties.

Aluminum mesh is available in different weights and is a great armature for sculptural elements.

Molds are available in a variety of sizes, shapes and motifs and are easy to use with polymer clay.

Bead rollers are great for making uniform beads and are available in lots of different sizes and shapes.

CUTTING AND MEASURING TOOLS

Unbaked clay is soft and pliable and can easily be cut into thick and thin slices as well as into various shapes. Baked clay is sturdier, but it can also be easily cut. Have a selection of clay blades and punches at the ready to make cutting clay easy. Always use caution when picking up clay blades, and never allow children to use them.

Clay blades can be used to cut both unbaked and baked clay and come in several varieties.

A **rigid clay blade**, like the Kato NuBlade, is used to cut slices off a block of clay and to cut into clay sheets.

A **flexible blade** that can be bowed, like the Kato NuFlex, is used to cut clay into an arc.

A **tissue blade** is very sharp and is good for cutting thin, even slices from canes.

A **wavy blade**, which looks a little like a French fry cutter, is handy for rippled cuts and makes interesting patterns when cutting into a stack of multi-colored clay.

Craft knives are great for detailed cutting or for cutting curved lines.

Pattern cutters and **punches** come in a large variety of shapes and sizes and are also great for measuring out uniform proportions when mixing colors.

Hand-held punches work well for cutting tiny, perfectly shaped pieces from thin sheets of baked clay.

Rotary cutters are used with a cutting mat and a metal ruler to cut straight strips of clay quickly and easily.

Decorative scissors come in a variety of patterns and can be used to cut both baked and unbaked clay.

PSST... HERE'S A TIP

If you find yourself having trouble cutting cane slices of uniform thickness, the Kato Marxit tool is a six-sided tool that leaves slight impressions along the length of a cane to serve as a cutting guideline. There are also some easy-to-use cane slicers, such as the Precise-a-Slice.

From left to right: clay punches (gold), clay cutters (silver), craft knife, clay blade, hand-held punches

TAKING CARE OF YOURSELF AND YOUR TOOLS

Always follow established safety guidelines when working with polymer clay. Polymer clay should never be ingested, so make sure to clean your hands thoroughly after working with clay. Unwrapped food should never come in contact with polymer clay, regardless of whether the clay has been baked. Any tool used with clay and any surface you bake it on should be dedicated exclusively to polymer clay and should never be used to prepare food. You can use disposable baby wipes to clean your pasta machine, your tools and your work surface. Water should never be used to clean a pasta machine.

PSST... HERE'S A TIP

Polymer clay can sometimes leave a residue behind on your hands even after washing with ordinary soap and water. However, slathering on hand lotion and scrubbing your hands with a nail brush removes all traces of the clay. Take a few minutes at bedtime to pamper your hands with a gentle exfoliator containing sea salt and natural oils.

FINISHING TOUCHES

Polymer clay's versatility makes it possible to apply countless surface treatments and textures to both baked and unbaked clay. It can be adhered to a multitude of surfaces and can be sanded and polished until it shines.

SURFACE TEXTURES AND TREATMENTS

It's easy to achieve beautiful textured effects in polymer clay. Rubber stamps are available in countless designs, and you can also impress fabric, seashells, rocks and other objects into clay to create interesting textures. My favorite texture material is 60-grit sandpaper. Use your imagination, and you'll be amazed at how you begin to look at everything you see as a potential texture material.

Alcohol inks are vibrant, fast-drying and highly blendable inks.

Paints, either acrylic or oil-based, also work well with polymer clay and are commonly used to create surface designs or as a medium to antique a baked and textured piece.

Liquid polymer clay adds a glazed look and can also be mixed with small amounts of oil-based paint or mica powders for even more variety.

Mica powders, which usually have a metallic or pearlized look, can be applied to both smooth and textured sheets of clay to create beautiful shimmering effects.

Pastel decorating chalks add a soft tint and are wonderful for adding a realistic look to faces made with clay.

Metal leaf and **foils** can be applied to the surface of unbaked clay or layered into a clay stack for techniques such as mokume gane.

> **PSST... HERE'S A TIP**
>
> Almost everything impressed into polymer clay has a tendency to stick, so it's important to use something on the surface of the clay to serve as a release agent. Armor All in either the liquid or the wipe form works well, as do water and cornstarch.

ADHESIVES AND SEALANTS

Although unbaked pieces of polymer clay will bond to each other during the baking process, you can use an adhesive to ensure that baked elements bond together or to adhere polymer clay to metal and other materials.

Super glue, also called cyanoacrylate glue, is used to bond baked pieces of clay. Since it bonds in seconds, make sure you have things arranged exactly how you want them before applying the glue.

Poly Bonder Glue is a wonderful polymer adhesion choice. It comes with a brush-on applicator and is formulated to withstand temperatures up to 300°F (149°C).

Polyvinyl acetate (PVA) glues, such as Sobo, help clay adhere to wood and other smooth materials. Let a thin coat dry clear before covering.

Liquid polymer clay is an amazingly versatile material with wonderful adhesive properties. It's great for adhering two pieces of baked clay or for joining baked and unbaked elements. It's also useful for attaching embellishments to polymer clay and can be applied as a sealant to protect surface treatments like metal leaf. Liquid clay must be cured to create a permanent bond.

Flecto Varathane Diamond Polyurethane is a water-based varnish that's compatible with baked polymer clay. It's available in a gloss or satin finish.

From left to right: Poly Bonder Glue, Repel Gel, inkpads, alcohol inks, liquid polymer clay and PVA glue

SANDING AND BUFFING

Because Kato Polyclay bakes with a nice sheen, I don't sand or buff much. However, certain techniques do require sanding and buffing to enhance depth, especially with translucent clay. Using wet-dry automotive sandpaper, I usually begin sanding with 400-grit paper and then move up to 600- and 800-grit sandpaper in a sink or bowl of water, rinsing well after each grit. A drop of dishwashing liquid in the water cuts down on the residue that can accumulate on whatever you're sanding. To add even more shine and depth to your piece, buff it on a muslin buffing wheel or polish it with a piece of soft denim. Buffing wheels can be dangerous if used improperly, so be sure to follow the manufacturer's safety precautions. If you don't want to buff, a polymer-compatible varnish adds a glossy finish. Future floor wax can also be used to add shine to baked and sanded clay.

Sandpaper

COLOR CRASH COURSE

One of the best parts of working with polymer clay is the unlimited color choices—with a little knowledge and practice, it's possible to mix virtually any color. Here's a crash course on the basics of color mixing.

There are three **primary colors**: yellow, red and blue. By combining these colors, you make **secondary colors**: orange, green and purple. Mixing all three of the primary colors in various proportions creates **tertiary colors** such as rust or olive green. Adding white to a color creates a **tint**. Peach, for example, is a tint of orange. A **shade** is created by adding black to a color. Navy is a shade of blue. Every color has a **complementary color**, and they are opposite each other on the color wheel. To mute a color, add a pinch of its complement.

When choosing a color for a project element, remember that the colors used next to it can influence the way it appears. An intense color can have a large amount of visual weight even in very small amounts.

I recommend using a color wheel to help you get started. There are countless books written on the subject of color, and polymer clay artists Lindly Haunani and Margaret Maggio teach fabulous workshops on color if you're interested in learning more on the subject.

It's best to start with small amounts of clay when mixing new colors. Also be sure to keep track of the color proportions you use so you'll be able to duplicate the color again. I recommend that you bake a small chip of your new color and use a permanent marker to write the color recipe on the baked chip.

color index

Over 1100 Color Combinations CMYK and RGB Formulas For Print and Web Media

JIM KRAUSE

"I cannot pretend to feel impartial about colours. I rejoice with the brilliant ones and am genuinely sorry for the poor browns."
–Winston Churchill

BASIC TECHNIQUES:

CANES, STACKS & PLUGS

Many of the techniques used in the projects in this book build upon each other. Simply start by mastering the Skinner blend, and all of the other techniques will come easily. You'll be amazed at how many wonderful effects you can create once you've learned a few basic canes.

SKINNER BLEND TECHNIQUES

The Skinner blend is named for its creator, the talented Judith Skinner. This is a very versatile technique that allows you to make a perfectly graduated blend using two or more colors of clay. The Skinner blend is the basis for several of the decorative elements and canes found in this book.

MAKING A SKINNER BLEND SHEET

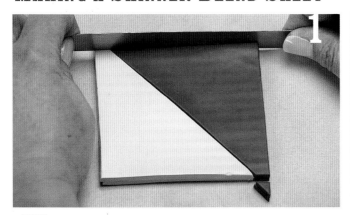

ONE
Create two-color square

Using two different colors of clay, roll ½ package of each at the no. 1 setting on the pasta machine. Trim each color into squares of the same size and cut each square from corner to corner on the diagonal. Stack the resulting triangles from each square on top of each other. Arrange the triangles into a square, offsetting them slightly. Cut off the corners of each triangle.

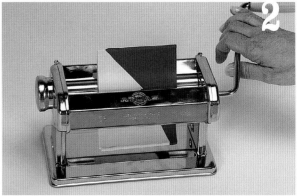

TWO
Begin blend

Press slightly on the two triangles to adhere them together. Lift the clay square from your work surface. Making sure both colors are touching the rollers, run the square through the pasta machine one time at a no. 1 setting.

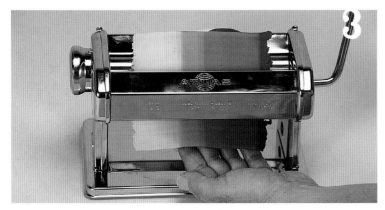

THREE
Continue blending process

Fold the clay sheet in half so that each color matches up with itself (blue edge to blue edge and green edge to green edge). Feed the folded sheet through the pasta machine at a no. 1 setting, fold first. Continue folding and rolling the clay, making sure to fold it the same way each time. You'll notice the colors here are beginning to blend.

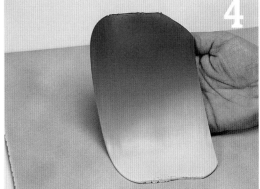

FOUR
Complete blend

After folding the clay and rolling it through the pasta machine about 25 to 30 times, you should have a blend that has an airbrushed appearance with pure color at both ends.

Skinner Blend Bull's Eye Cane

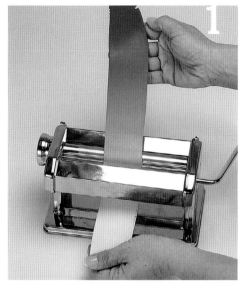

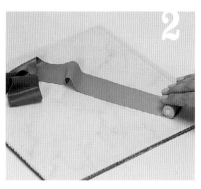

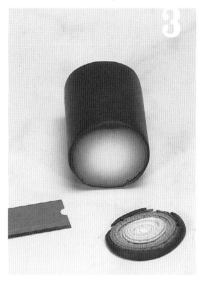

ONE
Lengthen and thin blend

To roll a bull's eye cane, fold the Skinner blend as before (blue edge on blue edge and green edge on green edge). With only one color touching the rollers, send the clay through the pasta machine at a no. 1 setting. Then roll the clay through the machine at a no. 2 setting, but do not fold it. Continue to run the clay through the pasta machine at progressively thinner settings, without folding it, until you reach a no. 5 setting.

TWO
Begin to roll up lengthened Skinner blend sheet

Lay the long, narrow blended sheet on your work surface. Use a clay blade to slightly trim both of the short ends of the blend. The color you begin rolling first will be the color in the center of your finished cane. Continue rolling until you've reached the end of the blended strip.

THREE
Trim ends of cane

Use your clay blade to trim the ends of the cane so the pattern is visible.

Skinner Blend Accordion Stack

ONE
Fold clay accordion-style

Follow the instructions for making a Skinner blend sheet (see page 14). Lengthen and thin the blend as shown in step 1 of the Skinner blend bull's eye cane instructions (this page, above). Use the clay blade to neatly trim the short ends of the blend. Starting at either end, fold the clay over about 2" (5cm). You now have the first two layers of your stack. Pick up these layers and fold them back 2" (5cm) in the other direction, as if folding a fan. Take care to smooth each layer with your finger to avoid trapping air bubbles. Continue until you've folded the entire sheet accordion-style.

TWO
Trim stack to reveal layers

Use a clay blade to evenly trim the edges of the stack so that all the sides are even and the layers are clearly visible.

SKINNER BLEND PLUG.

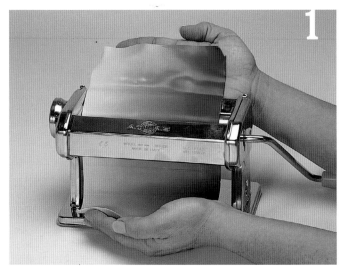

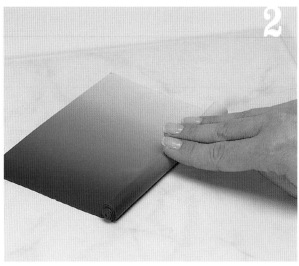

ONE
Thin Skinner blend sheet

Follow steps 1 through 4 for making a Skinner blend sheet (see page 14). Set the pasta machine at a no. 2 setting and run the blended sheet through the pasta machine with all colors touching the rollers. Don't fold the sheet. Continue running the sheet through the pasta machine this way at progressively thinner settings until you've reached the no. 5 setting.

TWO
Roll up Skinner blend sheet

Use the clay blade to trim away any uneven edges and begin to roll the thinned sheet from one multi-colored edge to the other. When you're finished, you'll have something that looks a little like a cigar with a different color at each end.

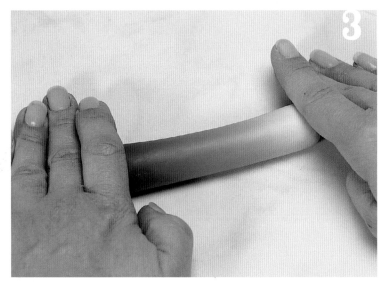

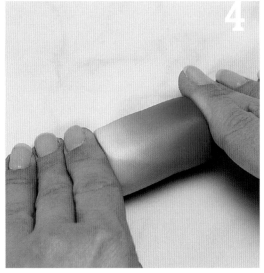

THREE
Begin to compress log

Compress the log by rolling it back and forth on your work surface. As you roll, your hands should be exerting pressure from the ends of the log inward toward the center.

FOUR
Create plug

Occasionally stop and gently roll the center to keep the cane smooth. Continue compressing until you have a plug about 2" to 3" (5cm to 8cm) long.

FLOWER CANE

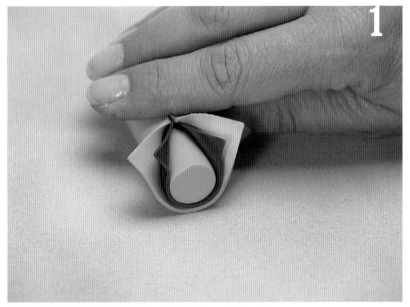

ONE
Create flower center

Pick a color for the center of your flower and roll out a 3" (8cm) long log of clay about ½" (1cm) in diameter. Roll a sheet of clay in a coordinating color through the pasta machine at a no. 6 setting. Trim a straight edge on the sheet with a clay blade and wrap the sheet of clay around the flower center log. Roll the wrapped log on your work surface slightly past the cut edge, then roll the cane back slightly and use a clay blade to trim away the excess clay at the impression left at the cut edge. Roll slightly on your work surface to smooth the seam. Roll a third color of clay through the pasta machine at a no. 4 setting and wrap this sheet around the log also, trimming away the excess clay as before and rolling to smooth the seam. In this photo, you can see how the flower center has been constructed with the different layers of clay.

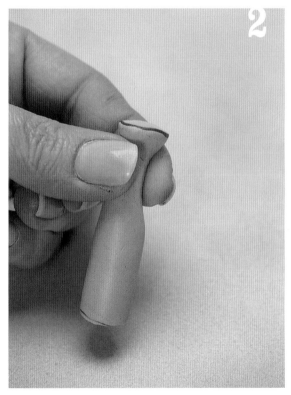

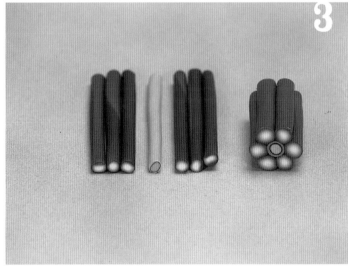

THREE
Create petals and assemble flower cane

Create a Skinner blend bull's eye cane (see page 15) using the colors you would like your flower petals to be. Reduce this cane just as you reduced the center section of the flower. You'll need about 18" (46cm) of cane ¼" (6mm) in diameter. Cut this cane into six 3" (8cm) sections to create the petals of the flower. Arrange the petals around the center section, pressing gently to adhere all of the canes together. Use a clay blade to cut thin slices off the cane to decorate any project.

TWO
Begin reducing

Squeeze the cane at both ends to begin the reduction process and then roll the cane on your work surface, using your fingers to smooth and lengthen the cane from the center out toward the ends. Continue the reduction process until you have a section ¼" (6mm) in diameter and about 3" (8cm) long.

BLACK AND WHITE STRIPES
I love the strong graphic element of black and white stripes, and I use them frequently in my work. This is a versatile technique that can be easily altered by varying the colors or the thickness of the stripes. When I make a striped stack, I like to make it large enough to use for several projects.

BLACK AND WHITE STACK

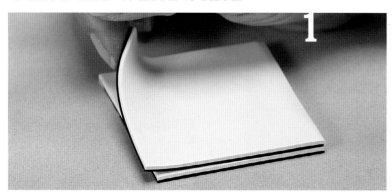

ONE
Stack black and white sheets of clay

Roll a sheet of white clay through the pasta machine at a no. 4 setting. (You can roll the clay at any thickness you desire—the thickness of the clay sheets will determine the width of your stripes.) Use the clay blade to trim this sheet into a 5" x 3" (13cm x 8cm) rectangle. Repeat with a piece of black clay. Place the white sheet on top of the black and smooth it into place with your fingers to avoid trapping air bubbles. Don't worry if the sheets are not lined up exactly—they'll be trimmed in a later step. Cut this rectangle in half and stack again, making sure that you stack the black layer on top of the white layer. You should now have a stack with four different layers. Press gently to adhere the layers together.

TWO
Cut, stack and trim

Cut the block in half and stack the pieces two more times, matching up the edges as closely as possible, and always stacking black on top of white. You should now have a stack composed of 16 layers. Press gently to adhere the layers together, taking care not to distort the stack. Use a clay blade to trim away the uneven edges from all four sides of the block.

JELLY ROLL CANE
The jelly roll cane is probably the easiest cane to make. I learned this particular way of constructing a jelly roll from the queen of caning, Donna Kato. It's a little different than what you may have seen before, but by constructing the cane this way, you'll always achieve a nicely balanced center.

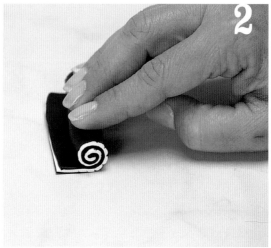

ONE
Prepare clay sheets

Roll out two sheets of clay in contrasting colors at a no. 4 setting on the pasta machine. Lay one sheet of clay on top of the other and trim into a rectangle about 2" wide x 4" long (5cm x 10cm). With the shortest end touching the rollers, run the two sheets of clay together through the pasta machine at a no. 4 setting. Fold this sheet in half. Use a clay blade to trim the uneven ends away, but don't trim the folded edge.

TWO
Roll sheet up

Starting from the folded edge, slowly roll the sheet up. Trim the ends from the cane to reveal the jelly roll pattern.

BLACK AND WHITE STRIPED SHEET

ONE
Begin to create striped sheet

Roll a black sheet of clay through the pasta machine at a no. 4 setting to create a thin backing for your striped sheet. Use the clay blade to trim the sheet into a rectangle about 2$^1/_2$" x 4$^1/_2$" (6cm x 11cm). Lay the thin black backing sheet on your work surface. Slice thin pieces off of your black and white stack (see page 18) and lay them side by side on top of the black backing sheet, making sure to always place a black stripe against a white stripe. Try to keep each slice the same thickness.

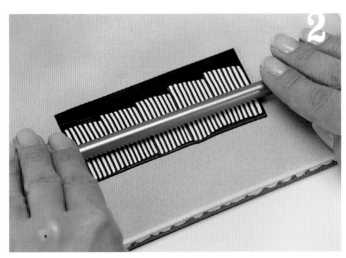

TWO
Embed slices

Roll firmly over the striped sheet with a metal knitting needle or brayer. You need to make sure you are adhering the slices to the backing sheet and to each other but you don't want to roll so firmly that you distort the stripes.

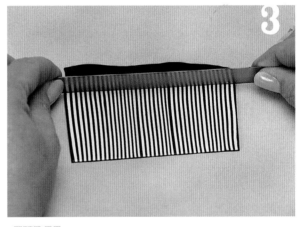

THREE
Finish striped sheet

Slide your clay blade under the striped sheet to loosen it from your work surface. Place the striped sheet on the rollers of your pasta machine so the stripes are running vertically. You want to make the stripes longer but not wider. Run the sheet through at the thickest setting. Continue to roll the sheet through the pasta machine at progressively thinner settings until you reach the no. 4 setting. Trim the uneven edges from the striped sheet using a clay blade. Simply slice pieces from this sheet as needed to embellish your projects.

JEWELRY AND ACCESSORIES

One of the most popular things to make with polymer clay is jewelry—and for good reason. The versatility and imitative qualities of polymer clay lend themselves beautifully to jewelry pieces of all kinds. Even better, polymer clay makes it possible to create fantastic jewelry and personal accessories in a relatively short amount of time. So take advantage of the instant (almost) gratification that polymer clay offers and expand your jewelry wardrobe with signature pieces that show off your personality.

In this section, you'll find some really unique and funky jewelry projects, like a flexible bracelet decorated with olives made of clay (what else!) and a fun and sexy torso pendant. There are also some great purse accessories like a little box for mints or pills and a bag tag designed to add a creative touch to your favorite handbag or tote.

PUNCHY MOSAIC EARRINGS

One of the best things about mosaic art-work is that there are innumerable possibilities. Different combinations of color, shape, size and arrangement appeal to different people, making every mosaic a personal state-ment. Use these fabulous hand punches on thin sheets of baked clay to make tiny mosaic pieces that you can arrange into a pair of stunning and lightweight earrings. Feel free to experiment with different colors, shapes and arrangements to make your own statement.

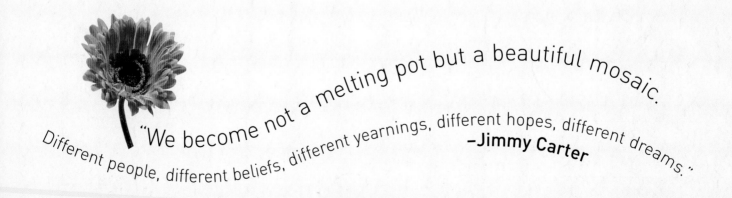

"We become not a melting pot but a beautiful mosaic. Different people, different beliefs, different yearnings, different hopes, different dreams."
—Jimmy Carter

WHAT YOU WILL NEED

polymer clay
　1 block black
　1 block green
　1 block yellow
　1 block ultra blue
　1 block white
　1 block violet
　1 block magenta

liquid polymer clay

Poly Bonder Glue

2 silver eye pins

2 silver beads

1 pair silver ear wires

hand punches
　1/4" (6mm) rectangle
　3/16" (5mm) triangle
　5/16" (8mm) diamond
　3/16" (5mm) square

3/4" (2cm) square
pattern cutter

texture plate
SQUARE PATTERN BY FISKARS

round-nose pliers

wire cutters

pin vise with .040 drill bit

index card or parchment
paper

release agent
SUCH AS ARMOR ALL

clay blade

tweezers

ceramic tile

small paintbrush

JUST FOR THE FUN OF IT...
the next dimension

I've included this little "bonus" feature for some of the book's projects to give you helpful hints and insights into the projects. I might warn you of potential pitfalls and/or mistakes I made as I was developing the projects. You might find helpful tips or ideas in this section or maybe just a personal experience I had while I was working on the book.

I have to say, I really love these punches and these double-sided texture plates! I have my to-do list written out for the year 2021, and at the top of the list is to make a mosaic tabletop entirely out of the tiny polymer clay pieces made with these punches. The earrings, though, are really quick and easy, and lots of fun to make. These tiny mosaics also look great embedded into unbaked clay.

Try covering a piece of scrap clay with imitation gold or silver leaf before you bake it. Then, when it comes out of the oven, punch out some glitzy little shapes and whip up a mosaic tiara.

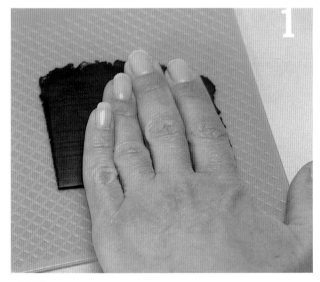

ONE
Prepare black clay

Prepare a small square of black clay by running it through the pasta machine at a no. 2 setting. Spray a little release agent on one side to prevent the clay from sticking to the texture plate. Lay the sheet of black clay on top of the texture plate and press firmly and evenly with your hand to impress the design into the clay.

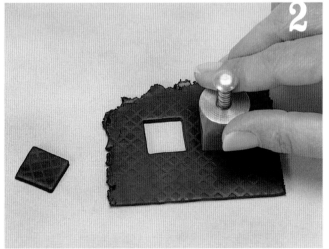

TWO
Create earring base

Cut out two squares from the sheet of black clay with the 3/4" (2cm) square cutter. Lay the two small squares textured side down on an index card.

THREE
Prepare clay for mosaic pieces

Add a small amount of green to the yellow clay to make lime and a small amount of ultra blue clay to the white clay to make light blue. Roll small sheets, about 2" x 1½" (5cm x 4cm), of lime, light blue, violet and magenta clays on the no. 7 setting on the pasta machine. Place them on a ceramic tile, and adhere them well by smoothing over them with your finger so that no bubbles develop during baking. Bake them for 15 minutes at 275°F. Let the clay cool.

FOUR
Punch out mosaic shapes

Remove the baked clay sheets from the ceramic tile. Punch 8 rectangles from the magenta clay, 8 triangles from the light blue clay, 8 diamonds from the violet clay, and 2 squares from the lime clay.

SIX
Re-bake earrings

Brush another fairly thick coat of liquid polymer clay on the front of the earrings. Bake the earrings again at 275°F for 30 minutes. Let cool.

FIVE
Adhere mosaic pieces to earrings and bake

Brush a thin coat of liquid polymer clay onto the black squares using a small paintbrush. You may use your fingers or tweezers to arrange the mosaic pieces on the black squares. Press gently to adhere the mosaic pieces to the black clay. Since liquid clay doesn't dry until it has been baked, don't worry about getting the pieces in the correct positions right away. You'll be able to move them around as much as you want. Use a needle tool to guide the pieces into their final spots. Bake at 275°F for 30 minutes. Let cool.

SEVEN
Drill hole with pin vise

Use the pin vise to drill a hole about halfway through the earring.

EIGHT
Add eye pins to earrings

Push the eye pin through the silver bead and into the earring. If the eye pin is too long, use the wire cutters to cut off the excess. Brush a little glue on the end of the eye pin and insert it back into the earring. Let the glue dry.

PSST...
HERE'S A TIP

A pin vise is a small, hand-held drill and is usually purchased with several drill bit sizes stored inside the handle. It's a wonderful tool for jewelry making since you can make small, precise holes in baked clay without worrying about the distortion that sometimes occurs when you pierce holes in uncured polymer clay.

NINE
Attach earrings to ear wires

Use the jewelry pliers to open the eye pin and hook it onto the ear wire. Bend the eye pin back into place with the jewelry pliers. Repeat for the other earring.

VARIATION Graphic Necklace

This coordinating pendant was made with the same pre-baked pieces of clay I used for the earrings. In addition, I made a silver sheet by applying metallic leaf over a small piece of scrap clay before it was baked. I embedded the punched circles into the unbaked clay and used my clay blade to cut out strips from the other colors.

THEY'LL NEVER KNOW IT'S FAUX
DICHROIC PENDANT

When you wear this shimmery pendant, no one has to know it's **not real dichroic glass.** Polymer clay is the great imitator—it can be made to look like any number of surfaces, from turquoise and mother-of-pearl to leather and metal. This easy technique makes it a snap to duplicate the amazing iridescence and depth of dichroic glass. You can choose from a wide variety of foils and powders to create the color combination that makes you glow. Enjoy the oohs and aahs that are sure to come your way, and remember—only you have to know that it's really a faux!

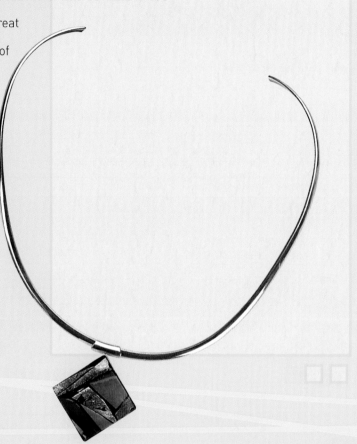

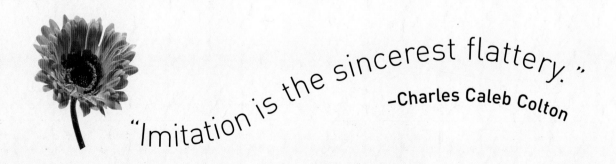

"Imitation is the sincerest flattery."
—Charles Caleb Colton

WHAT YOU WILL NEED

polymer clay
   1 block black

liquid polymer clay

Poly Bonder Glue

polymer clay foil OIL SLICK

pearl powders
   turquoise
   forever violet
   perfect gold

sterling silver bezel
setting

heat gun

polymer-compatible
gloss varnish

clay blade

ceramic tile

paintbrush

scissors

JUST FOR THE FUN OF IT...

irregular beauty

If polymer clay were to disappear tomorrow, I'd immerse myself in the magic of dichroic glass. Dichroic glass is formed by thin layers of different metals that are melted onto glass. The colors that result depend on the type of metals used. Because true dichroic glass is handcrafted, you won't see the same exact shape, color or pattern duplicated from piece to piece. Enjoy the irregular beauty of dichroic glass in all its variations.

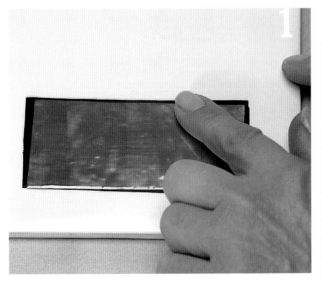

ONE
Apply foil to black clay

Roll a small sheet of black clay through the pasta machine on a no. 6 setting. Place the clay on a ceramic tile, making sure it is adhered well. Cut a small piece of the foil sheet and place it pattern side up on the clay. To get the foil to release onto the clay, rub your finger firmly and repeatedly over the foil. Don't press too hard, but do keep your finger moving back and forth over the foil very quickly to produce the heat and friction necessary to transfer the foil to the clay.

TWO
Peel away foil

Pull up one edge of the foil sheet to see if the foil is transferring properly. If so, remove the sheet from the clay in one clean motion. If there are large areas of black clay remaining, you may reposition the foil sheet over the clay and concentrate on burnishing over those areas to cover them. However, a few black areas are perfectly fine and will add interest to your finished piece. Bake on the ceramic tile at 275°F for 30 minutes. Let the clay cool.

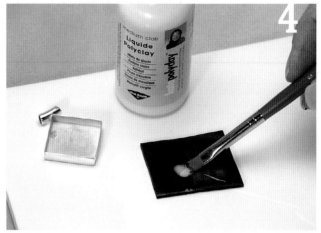

THREE
Apply pearl powders to clay

Roll another small sheet of black clay through the pasta machine at a no. 6 setting and place it on a ceramic tile. Apply the pearl powders to the clay with your fingers, blending them together as you go. Bake on the ceramic tile at 275°F for 30 minutes. Let the clay cool.

FOUR
Brush on liquid polymer clay

Roll a sheet of black clay a little larger than your bezel setting at a no. 3 thickness. Brush a thin coat of liquid clay over it.

FIVE
Press pieces into black clay

Use your clay blade to cut pieces of varying sizes from the baked foil and powdered sheets. Press these pieces firmly into the no. 3 sheet of black clay. Arrange the pieces randomly, leaving spaces in between each piece.

SIX
Set liquid clay with heat gun

Use the heat gun to set the liquid clay. Let it cool. Apply three more coats of liquid clay, using the heat gun to set each coat and letting the piece cool before applying the next layer. The heat gun will partially cure the piece so you can handle it without worrying about distortion. You'll bake the piece fully in a later step.

**PSST...
HERE'S A TIP**

When using a heat gun with polymer clay, always be sure to hold the gun at least an inch from the surface of the clay. Be sure to keep the heat gun moving so you won't scorch or burn the clay.

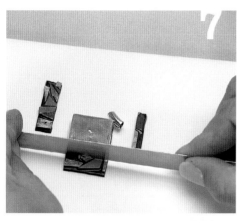

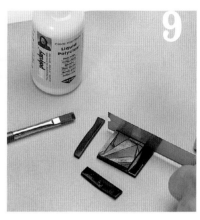

SEVEN
Trim clay to fit bezel

Lay the bezel upside down on top of the cured clay and use the clay blade to trim the clay so it fits nicely into the bezel setting. If the piece doesn't fit into the bezel exactly, keep trimming off small slivers with the clay blade until it fits snugly. You can also make very fine adjustments in size using a craft knife. Make sure to pay attention to the orientation of the cut piece so that you can remember which edges of the clay piece match up with which edges of the bezel.

EIGHT
Coat clay with glossy varnish

Remove the clay from the bezel and brush two coats of the glossy varnish over the piece, letting it dry completely after each coat.

NINE
Create proper thickness for dichroic piece

Determine how thick your piece needs to be so that it will be flush with the top of the bezel setting. Roll some black clay to the thickness needed, and lay the dichroic piece on top of it. Line up the bezel with the stacked pieces to see if the combined thickness is appropriate. (I used a no. 2 thickness piece of clay.) Separate the two pieces and brush a little liquid clay onto the black sheet. Press the dichroic piece into place on the black clay. Trim away the excess black clay.

TEN
Apply brush-on glue to bezel setting

Carefully apply the brush-on glue to the bottom and sides of the bezel setting.

ELEVEN
Finish piece

Place the faux dichroic piece into the bezel setting and bake at 275°F for 30 minutes. Let it cool. Display it on a sterling silver collar.

YOU'RE A GODDESS BAG TAG

The official name of the spunky lady used in this piece is "Nut, goddess of the sky." In a scandal of goddess-like proportions, Nut is said to have had an affair with her own brother (the Earth), and their resulting children became some of the most famous gods and goddesses in Egyptian mythology. There are thousands of other goddesses originating from far-flung lands rich with mythical legends. Each goddess possesses a particular strength or attribute, and each symbolizes feminine power. Embrace the power of woman in a lighthearted way with this funky bag tag. Check out clip-art books to find lots of great images (mine is from the Dover clip-art book *Egyptian Motifs*) or use your own artwork to make a truly unique statement. Of course you're different...you're a goddess!

"I have an idea that the phrase 'weaker sex' was coined by some woman to disarm some man she was preparing to overwhelm."
–Ogden Nash

WHAT YOU WILL NEED

polymer clay
    1 block white
    1 block magenta
    1 block black

liquid polymer clay

Poly Bonder Glue

black and white
toner-based copy,
approximately 1¹/₂" x
3¹/₂" (4cm x 9cm)

pastel decorating chalks

swivel hook with clip

2 metal beads with large
holes

thin leather cord, about
5" to 6" (13cm to 15cm)

texture plate FABRIC PRINT
BY FISKARS

¹/₄" (6mm) oval-shaped
pattern cutter

drill with ¹/₈" (3mm)
drill bit

rubbing alcohol

index card or parchment
paper

clay blade

scissors

craft knife

ceramic tile

cotton swabs

polyester batting

tricky transfers

Making transfers to polymer clay can sometimes be a bit tricky, so don't get discouraged if your first attempt doesn't turn out perfectly. A successful transfer depends on many variables that are sometimes difficult to control. The type of inks used, the age of the copy and even the temperature of the room where the transfer is made can affect the process. I recommend using a freshly-made toner-based copy for this technique, and I suggest you make two or three transfers at a time, just in case.

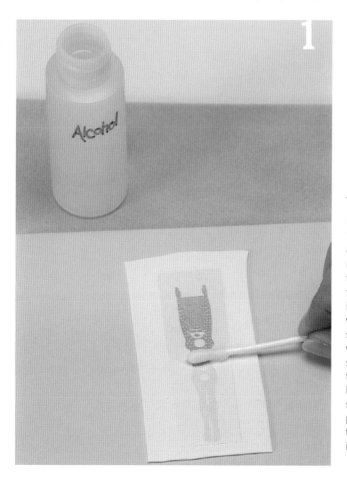

ONE
Transfer image to clay

Use scissors to cut out the black and white image you chose, leaving a ¹/₂" (1cm) border on all sides. Roll a piece of white clay at a no. 5 setting on the pasta machine to a size that is slightly larger than the image. Place the clay on the ceramic tile and make sure it's adhered well by rubbing over it firmly with your finger. Take some time with this step. Sometimes the clay appears to be well-adhered, but if you rush through this step, it will often bubble when baking. Lay the transfer face down on the white clay and burnish it well with your finger. Dip a cotton swab in rubbing alcohol and saturate the paper. Let it dry and repeat three more times. Bake the transfer with the paper still in place at 275°F for 15 minutes. Let it cool.

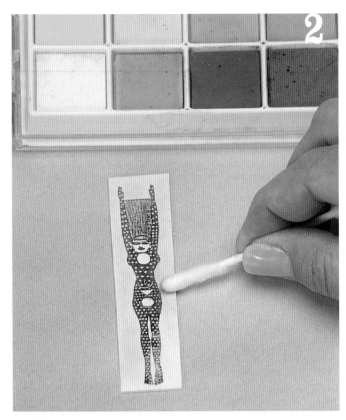

TWO
Add chalk to edges of transfer

Remove the paper from the clay and use your clay blade or scissors to trim the baked clay as necessary. Use a cotton swab to apply the orchid color chalk around the edges of the transfer.

THREE
Texture back side of tag

Condition a piece of black clay a little larger than your transfer at a no. 2 setting on the pasta machine. Make sure that the piece of clay is at least big enough to leave a $1/3$" to $1/2$" (8mm to 13mm) margin at the top of the tag so the swivel hook can be attached. Texture one side of the clay by pressing it onto the fabric print texture plate. Place the clay textured side down on an index card.

FOUR
Create frame for image

Roll a piece of black clay at a no. 5 setting on the pasta machine and place the baked transfer on top of it. Use the craft knife to cut around the transfer. Remove the transfer and discard the black clay cutout.

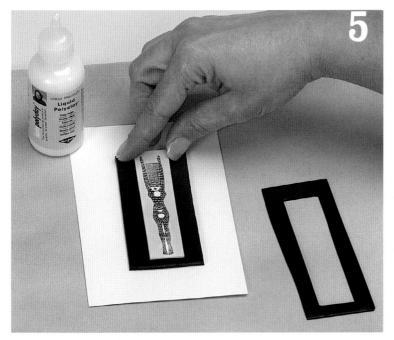

FIVE
Adhere transferred image to clay background

Brush a little liquid clay on the back of the baked transfer and center it on the no. 2 sheet of black clay. Press gently with your fingers to adhere it.

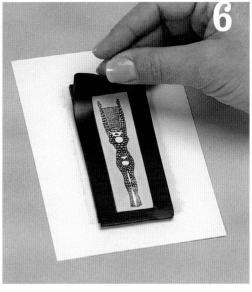

SIX
Place frame around transferred image

Center the frame of black clay over and around the transferred image. Gently press the two layers of clay together to adhere them.

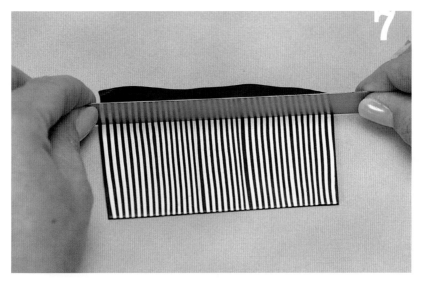

SEVEN
Create striped sheet

To create the black and white border, follow the instructions on pages 18–19 for creating a striped sheet of clay. Roll the striped sheet through a no. 2 setting on the pasta machine, and trim up the edges to make them even. The sheet should be at least $4\frac{1}{2}$" x 2" (11cm x 5cm).

EIGHT
Cover striped sheet

Prepare a sheet of black clay by running it through the pasta machine at a no. 4 setting and lay it on top of the striped sheet, making sure to smooth it carefully to avoid trapping air bubbles between the layers. Run the stacked sheets together back through the pasta machine at a no. 1 setting, keeping the stripes running vertically. Trim the edges with a clay blade to make them even.

NINE
Apply border trim

Cut $1/8$" (3mm) thick slices off of the border trim and place them around the edges of the transfer to create a frame. Use the clay blade to trim the sides and the bottom of the piece flush with the border. Carefully trim the top edge of the striped border, taking care not to cut through the black clay underneath.

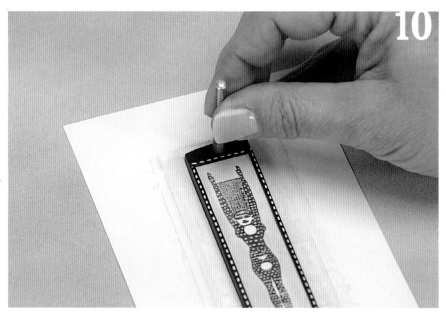

TEN
Punch hole for leather cord

Use the oval cutter to punch a hole for the leather cord near the top edge of the black clay. Bake the clay piece on an index card at 275°F for 30 minutes.

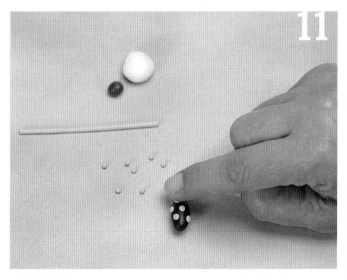

ELEVEN
Create bead

Mix a little white and magenta clay together and roll a snake about 1/8" (3mm) in diameter. Cut several tiny pieces off of the snake and roll them into balls. Form a 1/2" (1cm) ball of black clay into an oval and press the tiny balls of pale magenta clay all around it. Bake on a piece of polyester batting at 275°F for 30 minutes. Let it cool.

TWELVE
Drill hole in bead

Drill a hole through the bead that is large enough to accommodate four thicknesses of the leather cord.

THIRTEEN
Attach swivel hook to tag and secure bead

Fold the leather cord in half and insert the ends through the hole in the top of the tag. Pull the ends back through the cord loop and string on the beads and the swivel hook. Push the cord ends back through the first metal bead and the clay bead. If you're having trouble getting the cord to fit into the bead hole, taper the ends of the leather cord with scissors. Brush a little glue on the ends of the cord and pull the ends back into the clay bead. Let the glue dry.

PSST...
HERE'S A TIP

When baking round beads, you can suspend them on a wire or wooden skewer over a baking tray to prevent flat spots from forming during baking. Baking on polyester batting is another way to prevent flat spots from forming on items with a rounded surface.

FASHION FOLD
ENVELOPE EARRINGS

These lightweight earrings are a breeze to make, and the black frame sets off any color combination. Depending on the beads you pair them with, they can become as elegant or as funky as you like. Best of all, these fashionable earrings will be in style for far longer than one season. But if you're forward thinking when it comes to fashion, this might be a good time for color experimentation. Substitute a contrasting bright color for the black frame and see what happens. Try using complementary colors—refer to your color wheel and the color discussion on page 13 for more ideas.

"I base most of my fashion taste on what doesn't itch."
—Gilda Radner

WHAT YOU WILL NEED

polymer clay
  1 block violet
  1 block pearl
  1 block turquoise
  1 block green
  1 block black

1 pair silver earring wires

2 silver head pins

4 silver spacer beads

4 faceted glass beads (4mm)

2 glass seed beads

³/₄" (19mm) square pattern cutter

pin vise with small drill bit

round-nose pliers

wire cutters

clay blade

60-grit sandpaper

JUST FOR THE FUN OF IT...
pearly magic

If you're in a hurry and not feeling too particular about making colors in precise ratios, place a thin sheet of pearl clay underneath your triangles before you begin your Skinner blend. Complete the blend as usual and you'll get a blend with a nice pearl sheen to it. Try using gold or white under your triangles for a totally different effect.

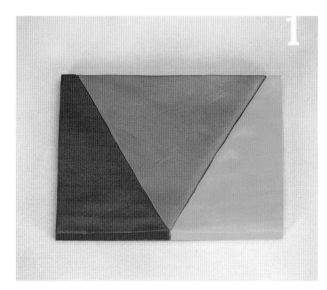

ONE
Make 3-part Skinner blend

To make a three-part Skinner blend, follow the same basic instructions for making a two-part Skinner blend, except you'll start with three triangles instead of just two (see Basic Techniques, page 14). I used violet mixed with a small ball of pearl, turquoise mixed with a small ball of pearl, and green and pearl mixed together in equal amounts.

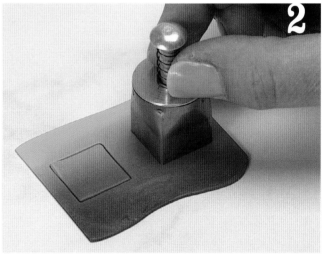

TWO
Create plug, punch out squares

Cut a small strip (about ¹/₂" [1cm] wide) off of the completed blend that contains all of the colors. Place the green end on the pasta machine rollers and thin the clay to a no. 5 setting. Roll this strip into a bull's eye cane. Roll the remainder of the Skinner blend sheet into a plug (see Basic Techniques, page 16). Cut a ¹/₄" (6mm) slice off of the plug and run it through the pasta machine at a no. 1 setting with all of the colors touching the rollers. Continue running the clay through the pasta machine at progressively thinner settings until you reach the no. 5 setting. Use the square cutter to cut out two squares from the sheet of clay, making sure all three colors are represented.

THREE
Texture black background

Roll a piece of black clay through the pasta machine at a no. 5 setting. Punch two squares out of the black clay with the square cutter. Remove the squares and set them aside. Place the squares you cut from the Skinner blend plug sheet into the holes in the black clay. Use sandpaper to texture the black clay.

FOUR
Create black border

Use your clay blade to cut out the two squares, leaving a 1/8" (3mm) border around each one. These squares will become the earrings.

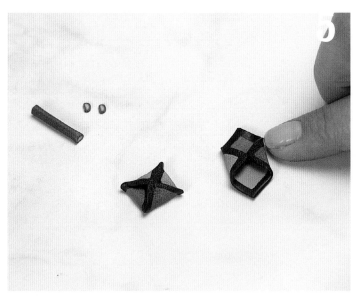

FIVE
Create envelope folds

Reduce the Skinner blend bull's eye cane from step 1 to 1/8" (3mm) in diameter and cut off two thin slices. Set them aside.

Turn the squares diagonally on your work surface and fold the two points on the sides in toward the center. Fold the top and bottom points in toward the center. Press lightly to adhere them, but don't completely flatten the folds.

SIX
Apply cane slices to earring centers

Place a cane slice (from previous step) in the center of each earring, pressing gently to adhere. Bake the earrings at 275°F for 30 minutes. Let them cool.

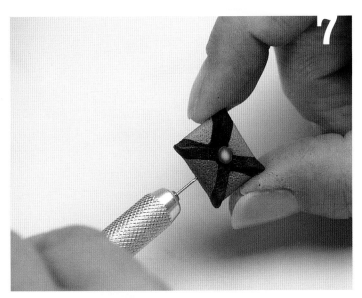

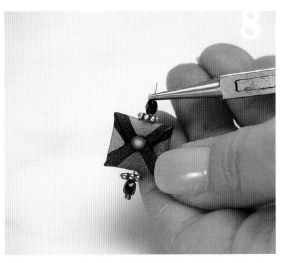

SEVEN
Create holes for head pins

Use the pin vise to drill a hole through each of the earrings from top to bottom.

EIGHT
String beads and clay earrings onto head pins

String one seed bead, one glass and one spacer bead onto the head pin, followed by the clay earring and the remaining spacer and glass bead. Use the wire cutters to trim the head pin, leaving $1/4$" (6mm) of wire at the end. Use the round-nose pliers to make a loop at the end of the head pin, but don't close the loop. Repeat for the remaining earring.

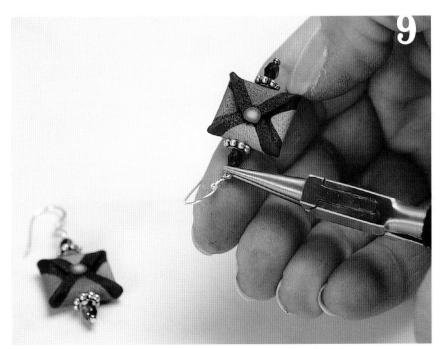

NINE
Add ear wires

Insert the ear wire onto the loop at the top of your earring and use the round-nose pliers to completely close the head pin loop. Repeat for the remaining earring.

POP-YOUR-TOP
EYEGLASS CASE

This great plastic pop-top case can be purchased in a variety of colors in the notions section of your local craft **store.** Since this type of plastic can withstand baking temperatures, it was begging to be covered in polymer clay. It's a stylish way to carry your glasses, scissors, clay tools or certain personal items that always seem to spill out when you drop your purse. Be on the lookout for new things to incorporate into your polymer creations. Shop with an open mind and lots of imagination. Don't be afraid to break the "rules"!

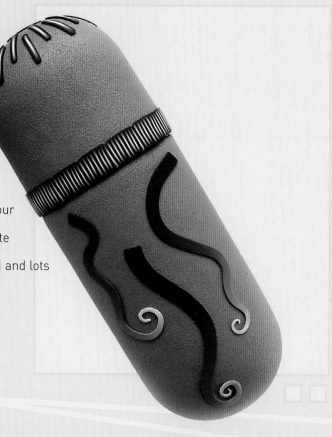

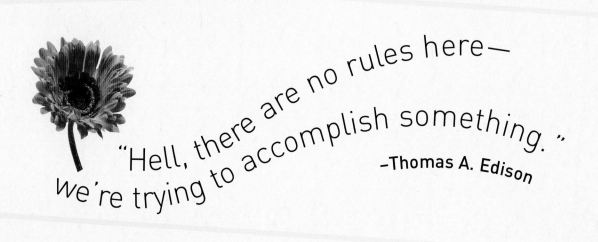

"Hell, there are no rules here—
we're trying to accomplish something."
—Thomas A. Edison

WHAT YOU WILL NEED

polymer clay
    1 block turquoise
    1 block pearl
    1 block green
    1 block black
    1 block white

plastic pop-top case DRITZ

fine needle

brayer

clay blade

60-grit sandpaper

JUST FOR THE FUN OF IT...
bake it naked

While perusing through my local craft store, I came upon these fabulous pop-top cases in the notions section. The first thing that caught my eye were the colors: bright blue, hot pink and purple. When I picked one up, I loved the fact that they were so smooth and that the lid really popped when it was opened. But, best of all, I was almost certain that they were "bakeable." As soon as I got home, I tossed one in the oven to make sure. As you experiment with polymer clay, you'll get a feel for what works in the oven and what doesn't. Some materials may not melt, but they'll warp. I learned my lesson several years ago when a wooden picture frame I covered with clay fell apart after baking because it had been glued together at the joints. So remember, never waste your time or your clay covering or embellishing anything until you "bake it naked" first.

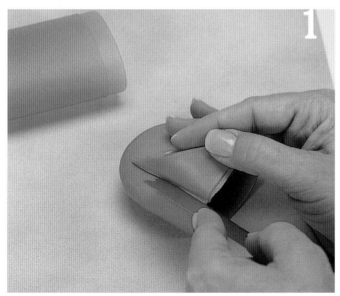

ONE
Cover case in turquoise clay

Mix 1 block turquoise, 1/3 block pearl and 1/4 block green clay and roll the mixture through the pasta machine until it reaches a no. 4 thickness. Separate the top and bottom of your case and wrap them with the turquoise mixture. Take care not to overlap the clay. Use your clay blade to cut away excess clay and pierce any air bubbles with the needle. As you wrap the clay around the rounded surface, it will naturally form a "dart," or a diagonal seam. Cut away this excess triangle of clay.

TWO
Blend seams together

Using your fingers, gently rub the clay along the seams to blend them together. Don't worry if it's not absolutely perfect because you'll be covering up any imperfections when you texture the clay. Check carefully, though, for air bubbles, and pierce them with a fine needle.

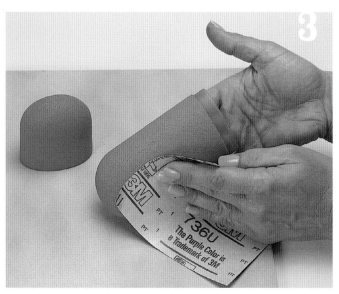

THREE
Texture clay

Texture the clay with the sandpaper or the texture tool of your choice. Trim away any excess clay after texturing is complete.

FOUR
Make black to white Skinner blend sheet

Make a black to white Skinner blend sheet (see Basic Techniques, page 14). Cut the sheet in half lengthwise with the clay blade.

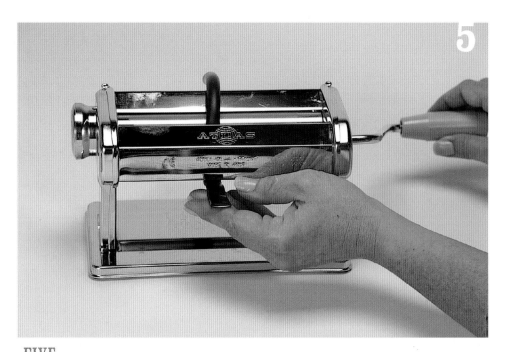

FIVE
Flatten Skinner blend bull's eye cane

Thin one half of the Skinner blend sheet by rolling it through the no. 4 setting on the pasta machine. Roll the sheet into a Skinner blend bull's eye cane (see Basic Techniques, page 15), and reduce the cane to $1/2$" (1cm) in diameter. Flatten one end of the cane with your finger and roll it, flattened end first, through the pasta machine at the no. 1 setting.

SIX
Create cane for border

Cut four 4" (10cm) pieces from the flattened bull's eye cane and stack them. Reduce the reassembled cane until it is 6" (15cm) long by laying it on your work surface and pulling gently with your fingers. Roll over all four sides with a brayer to keep the edges sharp. Cut the cane in half and recombine the halves by pressing them together lightly with your fingers.

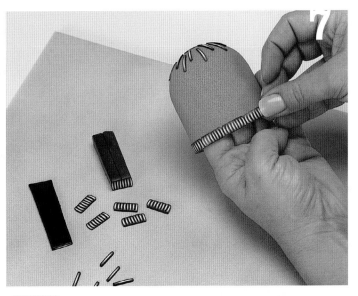

SEVEN
Decorate lid

Cut thin slices from the newly formed square cane and arrange them around the bottom of the lid. Cut thin slices from the remainder of the flattened bull's eye cane and arrange them around the top of the lid.

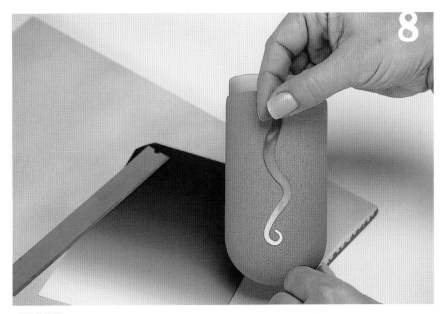

EIGHT
Finish eyeglass case

Thin the remaining half of the Skinner blend sheet to a no. 6 setting on the pasta machine. Cut thin, tapered strips from the sheet and arrange them on both sides of the bottom of the case in curvy shapes with spirals at the end. Bake the eyeglass case at 275°F for 30 minutes. Let it cool.

CURVY FEMALE TORSO PENDANT

There's something beautiful about the human torso. An area of great strength, it is also achingly vulnerable. The heart beats there, under the ribs, the center and life force of the body. Many of today's most popular workouts—like yoga and pilates—are focused around building strength in that area of the body, called core strength. When I saw this curvy torso mold, I knew it would make a great pendant. An object dedicated to the strength of the core of the body would be perfect hanging around a woman's neck. I'm happy to say that this project turned out exactly as I envisioned it. If only everything in life were so easy...

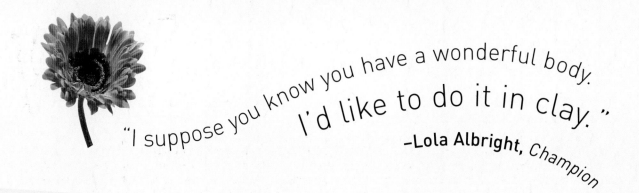

"I suppose you know you have a wonderful body. I'd like to do it in clay."
—Lola Albright, *Champion*

WHAT YOU WILL NEED

polymer clay
   1 block turquoise
   1 block violet
   1 block yellow
   1 block green
   1 block red
   1 block black
   1 block magenta
   1 block white

Poly Bonder Glue

small torso art mold
KRAFTY LADY

texture stamp VICTORIAN
LACE by HEART IN HAND STUDIO

28" (71cm) buna cord, 1/16"
(2mm) in diameter

1 no. 005 o-ring

silver eye pin

silver bugle bead

needle tool or pin vise
with small drill bit

wire cutters

clay blade

get moldy

The torso mold used for this project requires no release agent and its flexibility makes it a perfect fit for polymer clay. There are several molds on the market designed for polymer clay artists, but don't overlook the potential benefits of making your own molds from scrap clay or from commercial modeling compounds. Impress the object to be molded into scrap clay treated with a little cornstarch. Carefully remove the impressed object and bake the mold at the recommended temperature. Be on the lookout for interesting buttons, shells or anything with an interesting pattern or texture.

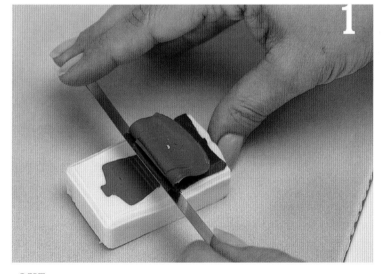

ONE
Mold torso

Using turquoise and violet clay, make a Skinner blend sheet (see Basic Techniques, page 14). Turn this sheet into a Skinner blend plug (see Basic Techniques, page 16). The plug will be turquoise on one end and violet on the other. Cut a 3/4" (2cm) thick slice off of the plug and press the clay firmly into the mold. (There is no need to use any release agent.) Trim the excess clay from the back of the mold with a clay blade, being careful not to slice into the mold.

TWO
Texture back of torso

While the clay is still in the mold, press the texture sheet into the clay to impress the pattern onto the back of the pendant. If the clay is sticky, brush it with cornstarch before applying the texture sheet.

THREE
Construct leaf cane

Make a yellow to green Skinner blend bull's eye cane (see Basic Techniques, page 15). Wrap the cane in a thin sheet of black clay rolled to a no. 5 setting on the pasta machine. Reduce the cane to $^3/8$" (10mm) in diameter and then use your fingertips to flatten one end of it. With the flattened end touching the rollers, run it through the pasta machine at a no. 1 setting. Cut seven 3" (8cm) pieces from the flattened cane. Lay one piece on your work surface and drape the next one over it, stair-stepping the piece so that the second piece touches your work surface. Continue draping the pieces in this manner until you have used all seven pieces.

FOUR
Create vein in leaf cane

Cut the stack in half so that there are two $1^1/2$" (4cm) sections (these will form the sides of your leaf). Lay one half of the stack on top of a sheet of black clay rolled through the pasta machine at a no. 6 setting. Trim the excess black clay so it covers the flat side of the stack, but leave the top quarter uncovered. Cut a second piece of black clay that covers the entire width of the flat side but that is a little shorter than the first piece of black clay. Lay this piece of black clay on top of the first piece of black clay. Layering the pieces of black clay in a tapered fashion makes the vein thicker at the bottom and thinner at the top, just like a natural leaf vein.

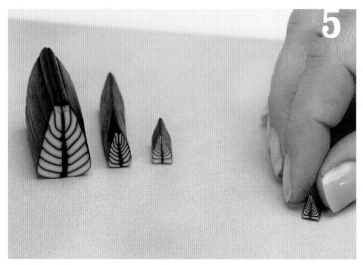

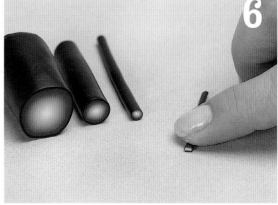

FIVE
Reduce leaf cane

Push the two halves of the leaf cane together carefully, making sure everything is lined up properly. Reduce the leaf cane by squeezing along the point of the leaf, using both hands to stretch it. Turn the cane frequently to keep even pressure on all sides to avoid distorting the cane. Continue reducing the cane until it is about $^1/3$" (8mm) in diameter.

SIX
Make berry cane

Mix 4 parts red and 3 parts magenta clay to make a berry color. Make a white to berry Skinner blend sheet and roll it into a bull's eye cane (see Basic Techniques, page 15). Wrap the cane in a sheet of black clay run through the pasta machine at a no. 6 setting. Reduce a small section of the wrapped cane to about $^1/8$" (3mm) in diameter. Flatten the berry cane into an oval shape by pressing it against your work surface.

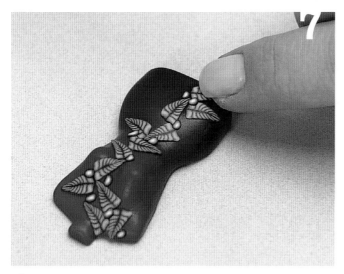

SEVEN
Apply cane slices

Gently flex the mold to pop the torso out. Smooth away any stray bits of clay from the edges. Cut several thin slices from the leaf and berry canes and apply them to the torso in a curving line from the top of the torso to the bottom.

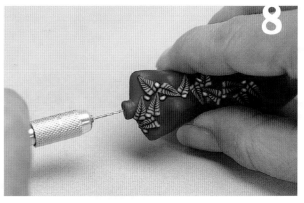

EIGHT
Drill hole for eye pin

If you wish, you can drill a hole in the neck for the eye pin with the needle tool before baking, or use a drill after baking. (I recommend using a drill after baking to avoid distortion.) Bake the pendant at 275°F for 30 minutes.

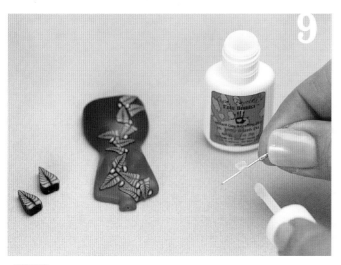

NINE
Make leaf beads, attach eye pin

Cut two fairly thick slices from the leaf cane (about 1/4" [6mm] thick) and make a hole in the bottom of each leaf large enough to accommodate the buna cord. Bake the leaf beads at 275°F for 30 minutes.

Thread a silver bugle bead onto the eye pin. Insert the eye pin into the hole in the neck of the torso. Use wire cutters to trim the eye pin as needed. Brush a little Poly Bonder Glue onto the tip of the eye pin and insert it into the hole in the neck of the torso. Allow the glue to dry.

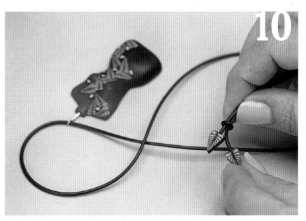

TEN
Adhere leaf beads

Thread the buna cord through the eye pin and push both ends of the cord through an o-ring. Brush a little glue onto the ends of the buna cord and insert them into the holes in the leaf beads. Let the glue dry. Slide the o-ring up or down to adjust the length of the necklace.

PSST... HERE'S A TIP

My favorite stringing material for pendants is a black rubber cord known as buna. It's often combined with flexible o-rings made of the same material and is available in different widths. Buna cords and o-rings are very strong and flexible—I've even been able to bake most varieties without any difficulties.

NO PRESCRIPTION NECESSARY PILL BOX

NO-PRESCRIPTION-NECESSARY
PILL BOX

Got a bitter pill to swallow? It happens to all of us now and then. To help the medicine go down, recycle a small metal pill box or mint tin into a stylish and colorful purse accessory. Feel free to experiment with your favorite color combinations and cane designs. Accessorizing may not be the cure for the common cold, but it's a great place to start. Feel better soon!

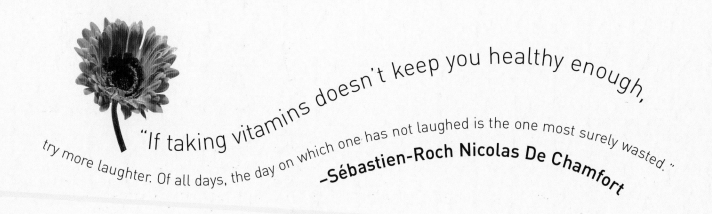

"If taking vitamins doesn't keep you healthy enough, try more laughter. Of all days, the day on which one has not laughed is the one most surely wasted."
—Sébastien-Roch Nicolas De Chamfort

WHAT YOU WILL NEED

polymer clay
  1 block yellow
  1 block green
  1 block violet
  1 block white
  1 block ultra blue
  1 block black
  1 block magenta

Poly Bonder Glue

small metal box

needle tool

very fine sewing needle

clay blade

60-grit sandpaper

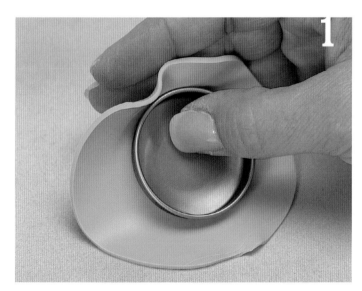

ONE
Cover box and lid with clay

Mix $1/2$ block yellow and $1/6$ block green clay to make a lime green
clay. Roll the mixture to a no. 4 thickness on the pasta machine and
cut out two pieces—one for the top of the container and one for the
bottom. Cover both the box and the lid with the lime clay, taking care
not to trap air bubbles under the clay. Pierce any air bubbles with a
fine needle if necessary.

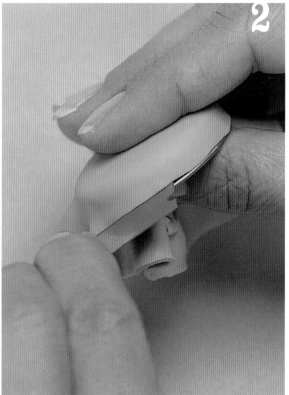

TWO
Trim clay to fit exactly

Lift up the edges of the clay and brush a little glue around
the perimeter of the box to make sure the clay adheres
well to the metal. Use a clay blade or craft knife to trim
the clay flush with the top and bottom of the box.

THREE
Texture clay

Texture the clay with the sandpaper or the texture sheet of your choice and trim again to remove excess clay around the edges or hinges of your box.

FOUR
Create Skinner blend bull's eye cane

Add a pea-sized amount of violet to $1/2$ block of white clay and a pea-sized amount of ultra blue to $1/2$ block of violet clay. Create a graduated violet Skinner blend bull's eye cane (see Basic Techniques, page 15).

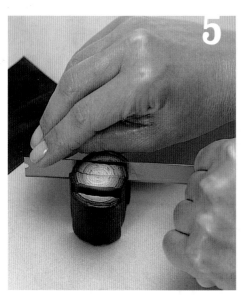

FIVE
Cut cane into quarters

Roll a small sheet of black clay to a no. 5 thickness on the pasta machine and set aside. Place the bull's eye cane on your work surface and cut it into quarters.

SIX
Reassemble cane

Lay each quarter of the cane on the sheet of black clay and trim carefully around each section, removing the excess black clay. Reassemble the cane with the pieces of black clay sandwiched between each section.

SEVEN
Wrap cane and create registration strip

Wrap the cane in a sheet of black clay rolled through the pasta machine at a no. 5 setting. Take a small piece of the violet blend and roll it to a no. 7 setting on the pasta machine. Cut a thin strip and lay it down the length of the cane to serve as a registration strip. As you reduce the cane, rolling it on your work surface, the cane has a tendency to become twisted. The registration strip will help you keep the stripes in your cane running vertically.

EIGHT
Create petal cane

Reduce the cane to $\frac{1}{2}$" (1cm) in diameter and pinch it into a point along the registration strip. Cut it in half and reassemble it with the points facing in opposite directions. Roll the cane slightly to round it and reduce it a little further.

NINE
Create different-sized petals

Cut your cane into three sections and reduce each to a different diameter to achieve the flower petal effect. Flatten and pinch each of the three sections into a petal shape along a registration strip.

TEN
Apply petals to box top

Cut slices from the largest petal cane and arrange them around the perimeter of the box. Continue with the medium and smallest petals, arranging them toward the center and between the larger petals.

ELEVEN
Add flower center

Mix a little magenta clay with a pinch of violet. Use the blunt end of the needle tool to make an impression in the center of the flower and roll several tiny balls of the magenta-violet clay to serve as the center of the flower. Place the balls into the impression you made and press gently to adhere them to the flower petals.

TWELVE
Decorate box bottom

Decorate the bottom of the box with a single petal slice and three flattened balls of the magenta-violet clay. Bake the box at 275°F for 30 minutes. Let the box cool.

FLEXIBLE MARTINI BRACELET (MARTINIS OPTIONAL)

FLEXIBLE OLIVE BRACELET
(MARTINIS OPTIONAL)

There are two types of people in the world—those who work on the fly and those who plan. The former play until they come up with something wonderful, and they're usually pleased. I've managed that a few times, and it's great. But I'm really in the latter group. I plan out every detail before I begin anything. Of course, things seldom go as planned—maybe that's why I trashed eleven olive bracelets before I finally made a perfect one. It was flexible, the thickness was right, the olives were arranged just so, and I *hated* it! I *never* wanted to make another olive bracelet and I didn't care if I even ate another olive. Ever. During the photo shoot, Jessica (my editor) said she had something to tell me. She was really, really sorry, but she had accidentally broken my perfect bracelet. I thought of the eleven botched olive bracelets in my shoebox at home and I felt like crying. But then I knew. I had worked out every single glitch. I *love* the olive bracelet again, and I hope you will too.

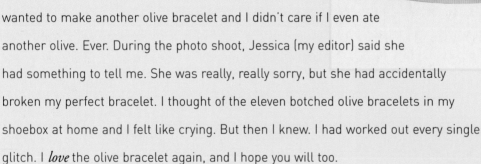

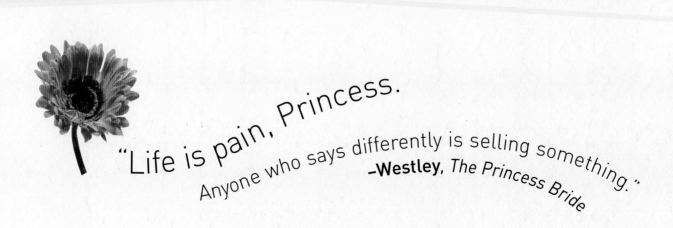

"Life is pain, Princess. Anyone who says differently is selling something."
—Westley, *The Princess Bride*

WHAT YOU WILL NEED

polymer clay
    1 block yellow
    1 block white
    1 block green
    1 block gold
    1 block black
    1 block red
    1 block orange

Poly Bonder Glue

cardstock or plastic
for template

$1/16$" (2mm) buna cord
(16" to 20" [41cm to
51cm])

1 no. 005 o-ring

oval clay pattern cutters
in three sizes:
$3/4$" (19mm), $5/8$" (16mm)
and $1/8$" (3mm)

needle tool

clay shaper or
smoothing tool

cardboard tube

scotch tape

parchment paper

cloth tape measure

clay blade or craft knife

ceramic tile

polyester batting

60-grit sandpaper

scissors

wonder clay

This unique bracelet is lots of fun, and it's easy to wear and remove because of its flexibility. (Just don't bend it completely in half unless you want to start your own shoebox collection.) Because both strength and flexibility are required here, I definitely recommend Kato Polyclay for a successful project. Its superior strength and flexibility can't be beat. Relish an olive, anyone?

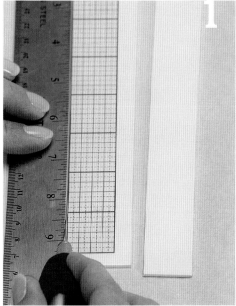

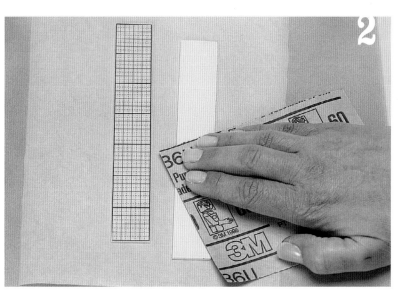

ONE
Create template and bracelet layers

Measure your wrist to determine how big your bracelet should be, allowing a little extra room so that it fits somewhat loosely. If your cardboard baking tube is too small, wrap it with sheets of cardstock and tape them into place. Then cut a template for your bracelet out of cardstock or plastic about 1" (3cm) wide. Mix a small amount of yellow clay with $1/2$ block of white clay and roll the mixture through the pasta machine at a no. 3 setting. Place the clay sheet on parchment paper and use your template to cut out two strips of clay using a clay blade or a craft knife.

TWO
Texture clay strips

Use the sandpaper to lightly texture one side of each clay strip.

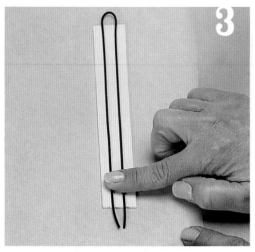

THREE
Place buna cord on bracelet layer

Turn over one strip of textured clay so that the smooth side is facing up. Cut a piece of buna cord twice as long as your bracelet with an additional 2$\frac{1}{2}$" (6cm) added on. (A 7" [18cm] bracelet would need about 16$\frac{1}{2}$" [42cm] of cord.) Fold the cord in half and center it on top of the clay strip. Leave a $\frac{1}{2}$" (1cm) loop hanging over one end of the clay strip, and leave $\frac{1}{2}$" (1cm) tails hanging off of the other end. Press the cord gently into the clay to adhere it.

FOUR
Sandwich buna cord and texture top layer

Lay the remaining clay strip, textured side up, on top of the buna cord. Press gently to adhere it to the bottom layer of clay. Texture the clay once more, pressing hard enough to further embed the buna cord into the clay, but not hard enough to see the outline of the buna cord through the clay.

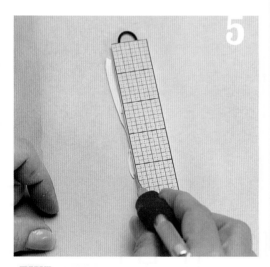

FIVE
Trim away excess clay

Use the parchment paper to help you flip the bracelet to its other side onto another piece of parchment paper and texture it again lightly with the sandpaper. (This side will become the front of your bracelet. Because it was pressed into the parchment paper, this side will be the smoothest surface on which to apply the olive embellishments.) Align the template over the bracelet and use a craft knife to trim away excess clay around the edges. Run a smoothing tool along all sides of the bracelet to smooth the edges together. You may also lightly texture the edges of the bracelet with sandpaper, if you wish.

SIX
Create olives and pimentos

For the olives, mix three parts yellow, one part green, $\frac{1}{2}$ part gold and a pinch of black. For the pimentos, mix 1$\frac{1}{2}$ parts red and one part orange. Roll each clay mixture through the pasta machine on a no. 6 setting. Adhere each sheet to a ceramic tile. Use the two largest oval cutters to make nine olives. Using the smallest cutter, make a hole in the top of each olive for a pimento. Use the smallest cutter to make nine pimento pieces from the red-orange clay. Pull the excess clay away from the tile, leaving the punched pieces adhered. Run a clay blade under the olives and pimentos to loosen them without distortion. Use a needle tool to remove the small oval from each olive and gently press a pimento into each hole.

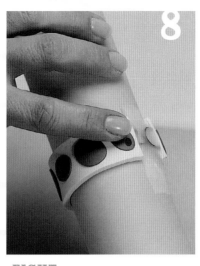

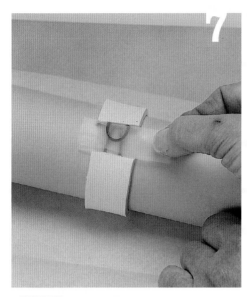

SEVEN
Prepare bracelet for baking

Lift the bracelet from your work surface and peel the parchment paper away. Carefully wrap your bracelet around the cardboard tube and use tape to secure the buna cord to the tube. Now that the bracelet is in place, you'll be able to add the olives without disturbing the texture of the clay.

EIGHT
Adhere olives to bracelet

Apply the olives to the bracelet, beginning in the center and working out toward the ends. I placed my olives at different angles so they look like they just tumbled out of the jar. Keep the bracelet on the tube and bake it on a piece of polyester batting at 275°F for one hour. Let it cool completely before removing it from the tube.

NINE
Create olive bead

Flatten a ball of olive clay and a ball of pimento clay to about 1/4" (6mm) thick. Use the largest cutter to make an olive and the smallest cutter to make a hole in the olive for the pimento. Use this small cutter to make a red-orange pimento and insert it into the hole in the olive.

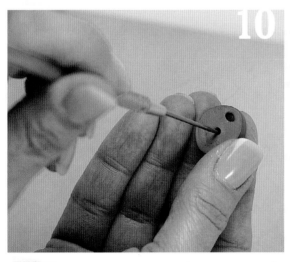

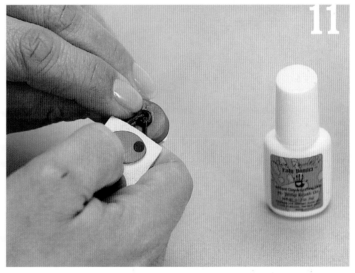

TEN
Finish olive bead

Use a needle tool to create a hole in the back of the olive bead that is big enough to accommodate a double thickness of the buna cord. Be careful not to pierce completely through the olive. Bake the bead at 275°F for 30 minutes and let cool.

ELEVEN
Finish bracelet

Trim the ends of the buna cord to about 1/2" (1cm). Slip the o-ring over both ends of the buna cord and brush the ends with glue. Insert both ends of the buna cord into the hole in the olive bead and slide the o-ring into place to hide the hole. Let the glue dry. Fasten your bracelet by pulling the buna loop over the olive bead.

NUDE WITH A
BLUE ATTITUDE PIN

I've always admired the work of modern painter Henri
Matisse. His bold use of color in sometimes unlikely combinations
has been a great inspiration. I've chosen his painting
Blue Nude 1 as the basis for this colorful
pin. The bright color and simple lines of
the figure lend themselves well to jewelry.
Using this fabulous color transfer technique
developed by Gail Ritchey and Donna Kato,
the color from whatever image you choose
will transfer vividly to your clay. To further
carry out the color theme in Matisse's image,
I've chosen to make a border of green and blue
cane slices. Matisse was never afraid to try striking new color
combinations, so go ahead and put your own spin on
this pin with the colors of your choice.

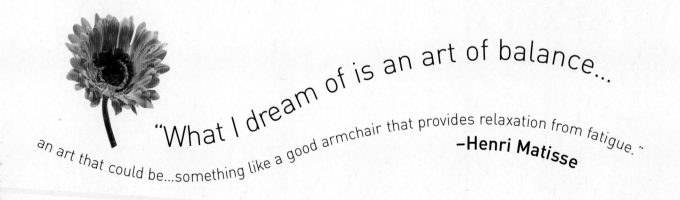

"What I dream of is an art of balance...
an art that could be...something like a good armchair that provides relaxation from fatigue."
–Henri Matisse

WHAT YOU WILL NEED

Polymer clay
   1 block white
   1 block black
   1 block ultra blue
   1 block violet
   1 block yellow
   1 block green

liquid polymer clay

Poly Bonder Glue

color copy from an inkjet printer

Epson glossy photo paper

texture stamp SWINGIN' SWIRLS pattern, HEART IN HAND STUDIO

1" (3cm) pin back

bowl of cool water

index card or parchment paper

acrylic rod or brayer

release agent

clay blade

craft knife

ceramic tile

paintbrush

60-grit sandpaper

scissors

ONE
Adhere image to clay

Select your favorite clipart or other image on the computer and print it out on an inkjet printer using Epson glossy photo paper. Remember to flip the image first, especially if your image includes writing. Cut out the copy, leaving a ¼" (6mm) border on all sides. Condition a piece of white clay and roll it through the no. 4 setting on your pasta machine. Place the clay sheet on a ceramic tile. Using a paintbrush, apply a thin layer of liquid clay to the printed image. Lay the transfer face down on the clay. Using an acrylic rod, roll firmly over the back of the paper in all directions. Make sure the transfer makes good contact with the clay—it's OK to distort the white clay. Bake the clay with the transfer adhered to it at 275°F for 15 minutes.

TWO
Remove transfer paper

Take the clay with the adhered transfer from the oven and drop it into a bowl of cool water. Let it soak in the water for about 15 minutes. When you see the paper begin to peel away from the clay, rub the rest of it off with your fingers. Lay the clay piece on your work surface and cut away the excess white clay around the artwork with a sharp blade.

THREE
Create background for image

Roll a piece of black clay through the no. 3 setting on the pasta machine to a size that's a little larger than your image. Apply a release agent to the clay and texture one side with the swirls texture stamp. Lay the clay textured side down on an index card.

FOUR
Create frame for image

Roll another piece of black clay a little larger than your image, this time using the no. 4 setting on the pasta machine. Lay the baked transfer in the center and use a craft knife to cut around it. Lift the transfer and the cut-out piece away. The remaining black clay piece will frame the transferred image.

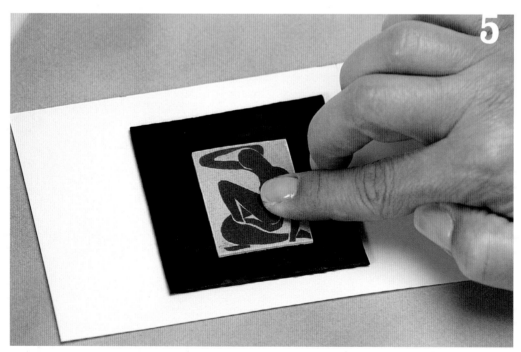

FIVE
Adhere transfer to black clay background

Brush a little liquid clay onto the back of the transfer and place it on the smooth side of the textured piece of clay. Press down gently on the transfer to adhere it.

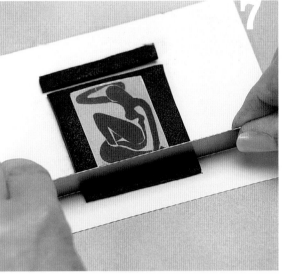

SIX
Adhere frame and texture

Place the frame section over the transfer to form a border. Use sandpaper to texture the frame.

SEVEN
Cut away excess black clay

Using a clay blade, cut a border around the transfer. Leave about $1/8$" (3mm) of black clay on the top and bottom and about $1/4$" (6mm) of black clay on the sides.

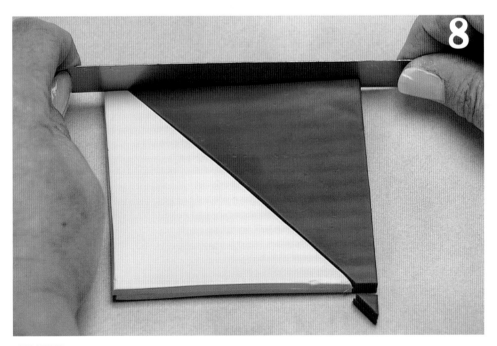

EIGHT
Begin Skinner blend sheet

Mix equal parts of ultra blue and violet clay (about $1/4$ block each). Add a small ball of yellow clay and an even smaller ball of green clay to $1/2$ block of white clay. Make a blue to yellow-green Skinner blend sheet (see Basic Techniques, page 14). Run a piece of each color of clay through the pasta machine at a no. 1 setting and cut each sheet into two triangles. Stack the green triangles on top of each other and the blue triangles on top of each other and place them next to each other on your work surface to create a square. Cut the tips off of each triangle to create a perfectly even square.

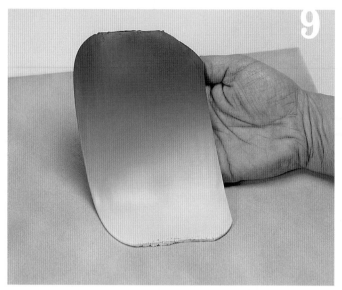

NINE
Finish Skinner blend sheet

Run the two-colored square through the pasta machine at a no. 1 setting with both colors touching the wheels. Fold it in half, green to green and blue to blue, and run it through the pasta machine again. Continue to fold the sheet and run it through the pasta machine at a no. 1 setting with all of the colors touching the wheels 25 to 30 times or until a graduated blend is achieved.

TEN
Create accordion stack

Lengthen your Skinner blend sheet by running it through the pasta machine at progressively thinner settings until you reach a no. 5 setting. Turn your long Skinner blend sheet into an accordion stack (see Basic Techniques, page 15). Use a clay blade to neatly trim away the uneven edges of the stack so that all of the layers are clearly visible.

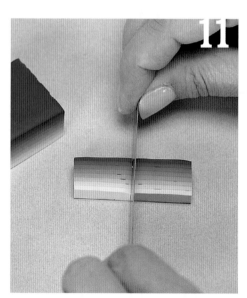

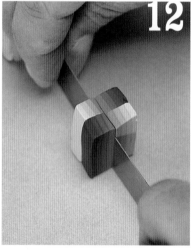

ELEVEN
Cut slice from accordion stack

Cut a 1/4" (6mm) thick slice from the side of the stack. Cut the slice in half, and stack the two halves on top of each other with the blue over the yellow-green and the yellow-green over the blue.

TWELVE
Cut block in half

Stand the block on one end, and use the clay blade to cut down the center of the stack where you can see the lighter blue color.

THIRTEEN
Create striped cane

Reassemble the block by placing the pieces side by side with the stripes alternating. You should see the lighter blue color along the bottom of the cane.

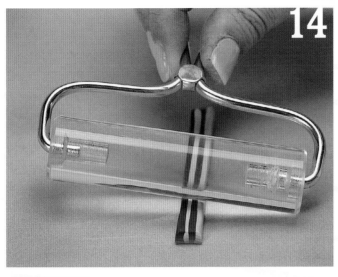

FOURTEEN
Reduce cane

Compress the sides of the cane with your fingers, taking care to keep the corners square. Lay the cane on your work surface and stretch it gently. Rotate the cane often and roll the brayer on each side of it to keep the corners square. Take your time, and continue the reduction process until the cane is about ³/₈" (10mm) in diameter.

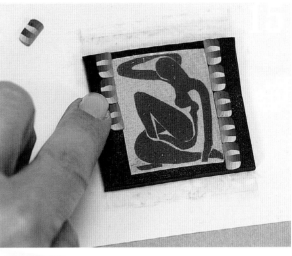

FIFTEEN
Decorate sides of pin

Cut thin slices from the square cane and place them on the sides of the pin. Trim away the excess clay from the vertical sides. Bake the pin on the index card at 275°F for 30 minutes. Remove it from the oven and let it cool.

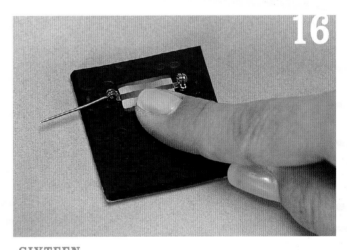

SIXTEEN
Attach pin back

Brush glue on the pin back and apply it to the back of the pin. Let it dry. Add a few drops of liquid clay to the pin back and apply a decorative cane slice to cover the pin back. Bake at 275°F for 30 minutes. Let it cool.

VARIATION Vintage Bicycle Brooch

There are several ways to transfer a color image to polymer clay. This pin was made using one of Lisa Pavelka's waterslide decals. The border was created with a blend of metallic clays and accented with diamond shapes I made using those great hand punches.

OFFICE
ESSENTIALS

Let's face it—going to work and spending the day sitting at a desk buried with papers is not most people's idea of fun. But surrounding yourself with a few colorful accessories may make those sometimes tedious tasks a little more pleasurable. At the very least, when your ink pen or letter opener disappears, you'll have no trouble spotting it on your co-worker's desk.

The best part of these projects, though, is that they're all truly functional things you can use every day. So, roll up your sleeves and get to work. I'm sure you'll be much more productive at your desk if it's decorated with a set of book-ends or a mosaic tile clock. And just maybe you'll take pity on your co-workers and make them some desk accessories of their own.

GRATED GOLD INK PEN

GRATED GOLD INK PEN

Yes, another ink pen covered with polymer clay! Technology may be advancing rapidly, but there will never be any shortage of work for the common pen. The one I use in this project is retractable and refillable, and you can actually carry it in your purse or pocket without smearing ink everywhere. A small spice grater makes it a breeze to add a sparkle of gold to a bright sheet of clay. Why not make one in every color? They're great for teacher gifts or stocking stuffers.

Write on!

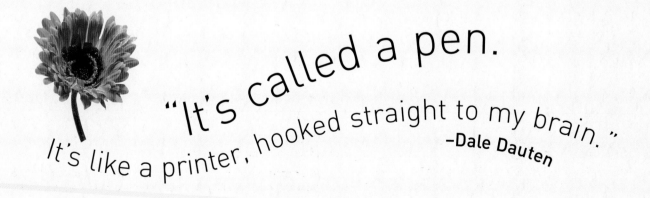

"It's called a pen. It's like a printer, hooked straight to my brain."
–Dale Dauten

WHAT YOU WILL NEED

polymer clay
  1 block magenta
  1 block red
  1 block gold

ink pen PAPER MATE
COMFORT MATE

nutmeg grater (clay-
dedicated)

white PVA-type glue

brayer or large knitting
needle

clay blade

JUST FOR THE FUN OF IT...
flashback

When I was in grade school, I had a friend who wore a necklace that I'll never forget. It was a glass vial of some sort that was filled with clear liquid. Floating around in this liquid were these amazing little shavings and slivers of what looked like hammered gold. I drooled over that necklace, and I've never forgotten it, even after all these years.

One day, while in my studio, I happened to pick up this miniature grater that was just lying around (along with 3,742 other things) and a small hunk of gold clay, and I started to play. It was like an instant flashback to the 70s, courtesy of polymer clay! I immediately saw floating gold in a little glass vial. Take the time to play occasionally. It's good for your soul!

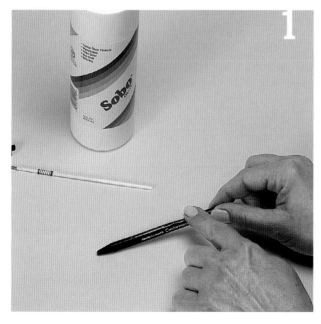

ONE
Coat pen with glue

Pull off the top of the ink pen and remove the ink cartridge and spring. Coat the pen barrel with a thin layer of glue and allow it to dry.

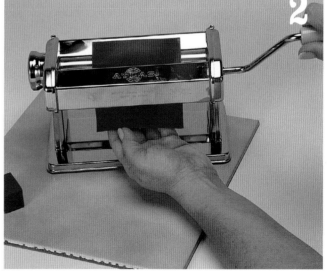

TWO
Mix and condition clay

Mix 3 parts magenta and 1 part red clay. Roll the mixture to a no. 4 setting on the pasta machine. You'll need a piece about 4" x 4" (10cm x 10cm).

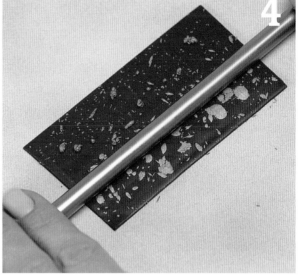

THREE
Shave slivers of gold clay

Cut a small piece off of the gold block of clay but don't condition it. Use the nutmeg grater to shave off small slivers from the block of clay.

FOUR
Add gold slivers to sheet of clay

Sprinkle the slivers randomly over the magenta-red sheet and press or roll them gently into place with a brayer or a large knitting needle.

FIVE
Trim gold-flecked sheet

Roll the gold-flecked sheet back through the pasta machine at a no. 4 and then at a no. 5 setting. Trim a straight edge on the sheet with a clay blade.

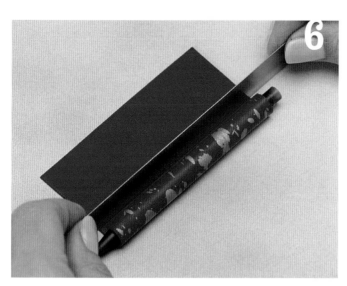

SIX
Wrap pen in clay

Turn the sheet over onto your work surface and lay the pen barrel along the clay edge. Roll the clay around the pen until it crosses over the cut edge. Roll the pen back slightly and use the blade to trim the clay at the impression.

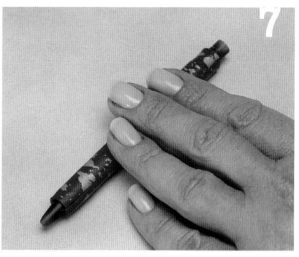

SEVEN
Smooth seam

Press out any air bubbles and smooth the seam by rolling it lightly on your work surface.

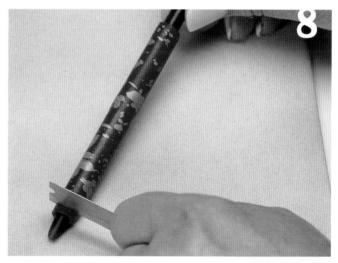

EIGHT
Trim ends of clay

Trim the excess clay away from the top and bottom of the pen. Bake at 275°F for 30 minutes and allow it to cool. Replace the ink cartridge, spring and pen top.

VARIATION **Purple Sparkle Pen**

This pen looks great in any color. Why not experiment with grating silver, pearl or copper metallic clays too? Of course, there are a million ways to wrap a pen in polymer clay. Play around and come up with your own unique spin.

LUMINOUS LETTER OPENER

Even if letter openers today are largely ornamental, it's quite romantic to have a pretty one around as a reminder, a hearkening back to days when letters were conversations between friends and lovers rather than bills, catalogs and credit card offers. Transform an ordinary letter opener of your own into an elegant desktop accessory using this quick and fun *mokume gane* technique. Maybe you'll feel inspired to begin writing correspondence—even if it's for the largely selfish reason that you'd like a letter in return so you can slit it open with your lovely new treasure.

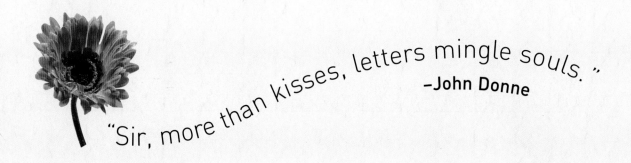

"Sir, more than kisses, letters mingle souls."
—John Donne

WHAT YOU WILL NEED

polymer clay
   1 block translucent

letter opener

imitation gold leaf foil

alcohol inks in red,
orange and yellow
SUCH AS PIÑATA INKS IN SANTA
FE RED, CALABAZA ORANGE AND
SUNBRIGHT YELLOW

found objects or tools to
make deep impressions
in the clay (golf tee,
shape cutters, wavy
blade)

muslin buffing wheel,
a piece of soft denim or
a water-based gloss
varnish

white PVA-type glue

brayer or large knitting
needle

clay blade

index cards

wet-dry sandpaper in
400-, 600- and 800-grit

cotton swabs or dispos-
able foam brushes

ONE
Apply alcohol inks to translucent clay

Roll 1/2 block of translucent clay to a no. 7 setting on the
pasta machine. Cut three 4" x 4" (10cm x 10cm) squares out
of the clay and lay them on index cards. Squeeze a few drops
of the red alcohol ink onto one of the squares and spread it
out evenly with a cotton swab or foam brush. Let it dry.
Repeat with the orange and yellow inks on the two remaining
clay squares.

TWO
Apply gold leaf to translucent clay

From the remaining translucent clay, cut out three more 4" x 4"
(10cm x 10cm) squares and cover one side of each square with
imitation gold leaf foil. Smooth the foil gently with your finger to
adhere it to the clay.

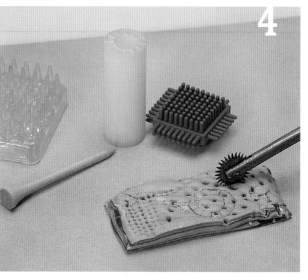

THREE
Cut and stack clay sheets

Begin stacking the clay sheets in the following order: gold leaf, red ink, gold leaf, orange ink, gold leaf, yellow ink. Cut this stack in half and stack again.

FOUR
Make impressions in stacked clay

Use the tools or objects you've gathered to make deep impressions into the top of the clay block. When you've distorted the arrangement of the clay sheets sufficiently, press the block gently back into place.

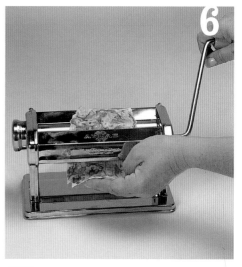

FIVE
Slice sections from stack and apply them to clay

Roll a sheet of translucent clay at a no. 5 setting, and make sure it's large enough to wrap around your letter opener. Anchor the stack to your work surface and use a very sharp clay blade to begin slicing off paper-thin sections from the top of the stack. Cover the translucent sheet with the slices, taking care to roll them smoothly into place with a brayer or a large knitting needle. You'll want to build up two to three layers of slices to add depth to your design.

SIX
Thin out clay sheet

When the slices are smoothly rolled into place, run this sheet through the pasta machine at a no. 3 setting. Turn it a quarter of a turn and roll it through the pasta machine at a no. 4 setting.

SEVEN
Wrap handle with clay

Apply a thin coat of glue to the handle of the letter opener and let it dry completely. Wrap the handle of the letter opener with the clay sheet. Trim away the excess clay and smooth the seams. Bake at 275°F for 30 minutes. Let it cool.

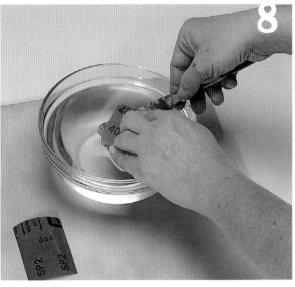

EIGHT
Sand handle

Sand the handle of the letter opener by placing it in a dish or sink of warm water with a few drops of dishwashing liquid. Sand the handle first with the 400-grit sandpaper, followed by the 600- and 800-grit. Rinse the sanding residue off of the handle and dry well.

NINE
Polish handle or add varnish

You may choose to buff the handle with a muslin buffing wheel or use a soft piece of old denim to polish it. Another choice would be to add a coat of water-based varnish for a glossy shine.

PSST... HERE'S A TIP

When using two or more different grits of sandpaper, it's easy to forget which one is which—and using the wrong grit can cause damage to your work. To help you keep it straight, simply turn your sandpaper over and write the grit several times on the back with a permanent marker. This way, even if you cut your sandpaper into small sheets, you'll always be able to tell what grit you're using.

VARIATION **Pencil Cup and Business Card Holder**

Use the same technique as for the letter opener to make additional desk accessories, such as a business card holder and a pencil cup.

GOT IT COVERED
ART JOURNAL

GOT-IT-COVERED
ART JOURNAL

I'm always sketching out ideas and jotting down notes for future projects. Putting things down on paper helps me think through the details of an idea and inspires me to keep creating. After seeing polymer clay artist Terry Lee Czechowski's journal, I was inspired to make my own. To make this art journal, I purchased a wire-bound notebook from my local dollar store and simply replaced the front and back covers with ones created from polymer clay. Add some images from your favorite rubber stamps to personalize your journal. The covers for the journal need to be both strong and very flexible so I highly recommend using Kato Polyclay for the best results. When you're finished, don't forget the most important part—keeping track of your ideas on the pages of your brand new art journal.

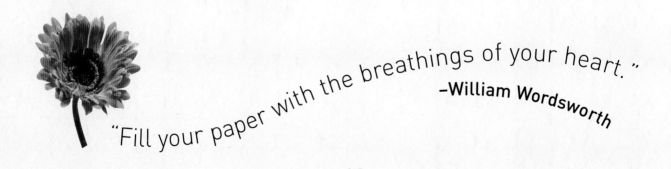

"Fill your paper with the breathings of your heart."
—William Wordsworth

WHAT YOU WILL NEED

polymer clay
  1 block ultra blue
  1 block gold
  1 block white
  1 block copper
  1 block pearl
  1 block turquoise
  1 block green
  1 block violet
  1 block yellow

scrap clay (about 8 oz)

liquid polymer clay

Poly Bonder Glue

wire-bound notebook

metal confetti or other flat metal charms

assorted rubber stamps TEESHA MOORE

black pigment ink pad

olive solvent ink pad

texture sheet LINEN PATTERN BY SHADE-TEX

1/4" (6mm) square pattern cutter

3/16" (5mm) circle pattern cutter

small clips or clamps to hold paper together

needle tool

release agent

clay blade

craft knife

ceramic tile

small paintbrush

JUST FOR THE FUN OF IT...
scrappy

As you continue to work with polymer clay, you'll eventually begin to accumulate what is known as scrap clay or "mud." While these bits and pieces of clay may not look too nice when they're all mixed together, I've mixed some of my favorite colors using a few pinches of "mud" or adding metallic clays to my scrap pile.

Another way to make use of your scrap clay is to use it underneath a thinner layer of color or pattern when you're covering an object or creating a sculptural piece. It's great as a base for lots of things, and you'll even find scrap clay for sale on online auction sites. There's never any waste with polymer clay!

ONE
Remove journal covers

Remove the front and back covers from the journal by slightly bending the wire coils. The covers will become the templates for the new polymer clay covers you'll create.

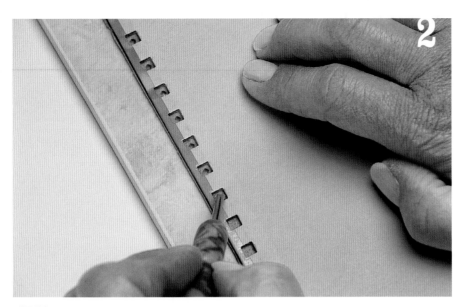

TWO
Mark hole placement for covers

This project is great for using up scrap clay. To make this blue-gray color, I mixed a bit of ultra blue, gold and white in with my scrap pile. Feel free to create your own color. Roll two large pieces of clay through the pasta machine at a no. 3 setting until they are a little larger than the notebook covers. Place them on a ceramic tile and adhere them well. Then spray a little of the release agent onto each sheet of clay and place the texture sheet on top of each. Rub firmly and evenly over the texture sheet to transfer the pattern.

Lay the front cover on top of one of the sheets and use a needle tool or a stylus to mark the placement of the holes for the spiral binding. Repeat with the back cover. Remember to make the holes for the front cover on the left and the holes for the back cover on the right.

THREE
Cut out squares for binding

Use the square cutter to make the holes for the front cover. Remove the excess clay using a needle tool or the tip of a craft knife.

FOUR
Create stamped embellishments

Decide what stamps and colors of clay you'll be using to decorate your notebook. I made a pumpkin color using copper, gold and pearl; I made a turquoise color with turquoise and green; I made a dusty plum color using violet mixed with a little scrap clay; and I made a lime color by mixing green and yellow with a little scrap clay. Roll your color choices through the pasta machine at a no. 5 setting and place them on a ceramic tile. Stamp your images onto the clay using black pigment ink. You may also highlight some of the raised areas on the stamped images with olive ink. Use a small circle cutter to make a few tiny circles.

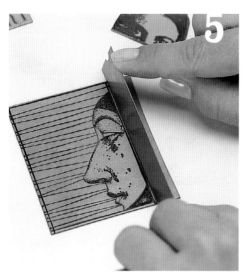

FIVE
Trim stamped images

Trim around your stamped images using a clay blade for larger straight edges and a craft knife for small or curved areas. Cut a few small pieces from a black and white striped sheet (see Basic Techniques, page 19), and place them on the ceramic tile as well. Bake all of the clay embellishments on the ceramic tile at 275°F for 30 minutes. Let them cool.

SIX
Apply stamped images to journal cover

Determine where your stamped images should be placed and brush a little of the liquid clay onto the backs of the baked pieces. Gently press them into place on the unbaked clay cover.

SEVEN
Apply additional embellishments

Fill in any empty spaces on the journal cover with the circles and the striped pieces. Add a few pieces of the metal confetti or some flat charms of your choice, pushing them firmly into the clay to make an impression.

EIGHT
Complete covers and bake

Personalize your journal by stamping your name into a small piece of clay and applying it to the back cover. Add other small embellishments, as desired. Bake the front and back covers of the journal on ceramic tiles at 275°F for 30 minutes. Let them cool. Gently pry the metal confetti off of the covers and brush a little glue onto the back of each piece. Replace them into their spots on the covers. Let the glue dry.

NINE
Reassemble journal

To reassemble the notebook, first clip the pages together using the clamps and slide the pages off of the metal coil. Then place the back cover onto the metal coil. Add the notebook pages and remove the clamps. Finally, replace the front cover, bending the coils back into place if necessary.

THE COLOR OF MUSIC
BOOKENDS

For me, music and color go hand-in-hand. I used to wonder if it was normal to see colors in my head when I listened to music. After doing a little research, I discovered that the idea of a link between color and music has quite a long history, intriguing even Sir Isaac Newton. I was happy to discover that one of my favorite artists, Wassily Kandinsky, considered to be the founder of abstract art, felt that music and color were almost one and the same. He even claimed that when he saw color he heard music. My fascination with his dramatic and colorful art resulted in these bookends, which are a breeze to create. So put on some music, break out the clay, and get started!

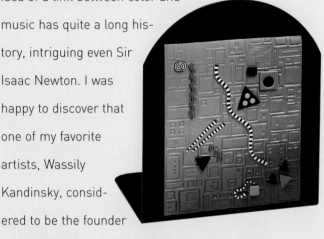

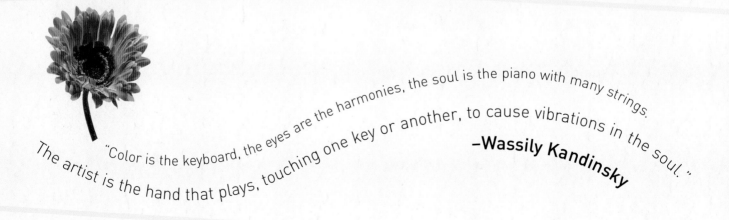

"Color is the keyboard, the eyes are the harmonies, the soul is the piano with many strings. The artist is the hand that plays, touching one key or another, to cause vibrations in the soul."

–Wassily Kandinsky

WHAT YOU WILL NEED

polymer clay
    1 block turquoise
    1 block white
    1 block green
    1 block pearl
    1 block gold
    1 block ultra blue
    1 block black
    1 block red
    1 block violet

liquid polymer clay

set of metal bookends

large background
rubber stamp METROPOLIS
BY JUDIKINS

assorted clay pattern
cutters

wavy blade

clay blade

ceramic tiles

release agent

paintbrush

60-grit sandpaper

JUST FOR THE FUN OF IT...
artsy fartsy

I love this project, and it was so much fun to put together. Here are a few things to keep in mind, though. Use fairly subtle colors for the background and don't feel you have to completely fill up the space. Negative space can be a valuable part of your design. If you use only one really bold color, such as red, it will have more of an impact than if you use three or four bold colors together. Learning more about abstract art is a great way to increase your understanding of design principles, and now you'll have a great pair of bookends to hold all those art books.

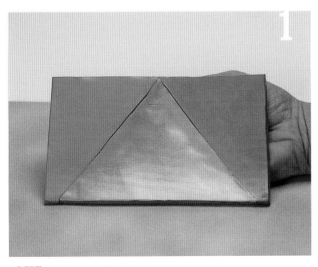

ONE
Begin three-part Skinner blend

Make a large Skinner blend using three colors. For the first triangle, I mixed equal amounts of turquoise, white and green and added a little pearl for sparkle. The middle triangle is gold and the third triangle is composed of equal amounts of green and gold with a bit of ultra blue. Assemble the triangles as shown and make a Skinner blend sheet (see Basic Techniques, page 14). Thin the Skinner blend by rolling it through the pasta machine at a no. 3 setting.

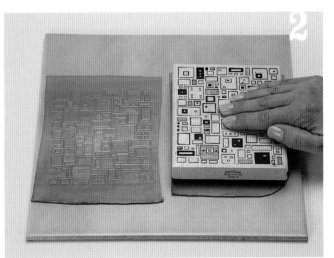

TWO
Stamp and bake clay sheets

Cut the blend in half and place each sheet of clay on a ceramic tile. Burnish each one thoroughly with your finger to make sure it is adhered well and that there are no air bubbles under the clay. Spray a release agent onto the clay sheet and press the rubber stamp firmly into the clay, making sure you've transferred the image completely. Remove the stamp and use a clay blade to trim around the stamped image. Repeat this process for the other half of the Skinner blend sheet. Bake both pieces on the ceramic tiles at 275°F for 30 minutes. Let them cool.

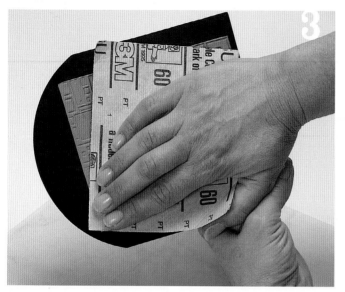

THREE
Adhere clay sheets and create black border

Brush a coat of liquid clay on the back of the baked and stamped sheets. Center a sheet on each of the metal bookends. Roll a sheet of black clay through the pasta machine at a no. 3 setting and cut it into strips to fit around the outer edges of the bookends. Make sure the black clay border meets the edges of the colored clay sheets as closely as possible. Smooth the seams with your fingers and use the 60-grit sandpaper to texture the black clay.

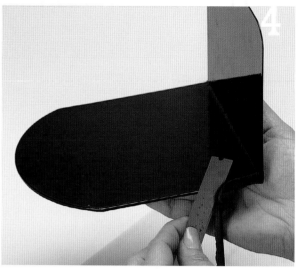

FOUR
Trim away excess clay

Use the clay blade to trim the excess clay from the edges of the bookends.

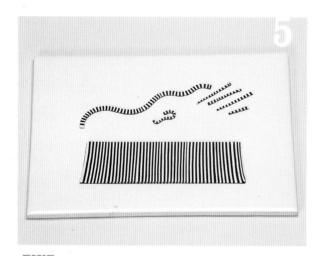

FIVE
Create black and white accents

Create a black and white striped sheet (see Basic Techniques, page 19) or use one left over from another project. Cut off thin sections from the sheet and arrange them on a ceramic tile in the shapes you like. Bake at 275°F for 30 minutes. Let the shapes cool.

PSST... HERE'S A TIP

If your three-color Skinner blend sheet isn't quite big enough to make two pieces that can accommodate the stamp, don't make a whole new Skinner blend sheet. Simply add a sheet of scrap clay that has been run through the pasta machine at a no. 3 setting underneath the blend and run the stacked sheets through the pasta machine until you reach the no. 3 setting again. The added clay underneath the blend will help to widen and elongate the clay sheet enough to accommodate two stamped images.

SIX
Create jelly roll

Create a black and white jelly roll (see Basic Techniques, page 18). Reduce the cane to various sizes (see Basic Techniques, page 17) and cut a few slices to add to your bookends.

SEVEN
Cut out colorful shapes

Roll small sheets of the remaining colors of clay at a no. 5 setting on the pasta machine. Use the clay cutters and the wavy blade to cut various geometric shapes.

EIGHT
Finish shapes

Mix and match colors and shapes so that you have squares with circles in their centers, triangles with squares in the middle, and so on. Use your imagination to come up with various shape and color combinations. Bake these shapes and the jelly roll slices on a ceramic tile at 275°F for 30 minutes. Let the shapes cool.

NINE
Adhere shapes to bookends to finish

Begin arranging the baked pieces on the bookends until you have a composition that's pleasing to you. Brush a little liquid clay onto the back of each piece and lay it into place. Bake the bookends at 275°F for 30 minutes. Let them cool.

NEVER-NEEDS-WATERING
HYDRANGEA PAPERWEIGHT

NEVER-NEEDS-WATERING
HYDRANGEA PAPERWEIGHT

What could be more beautiful than a hydrangea bush in full bloom? Keep the gorgeous colors blooming in your home or office year round by combining a beautiful blend of clay and an inexpensive glass paperweight with a few simple techniques and tools. Your hydrangea bloom paperweight will become your little oasis amid the clutter and confusion of your desk.

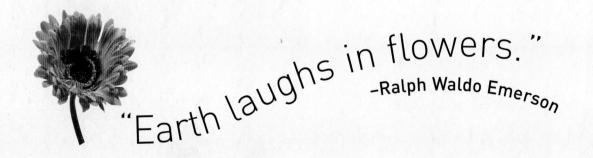

"Earth laughs in flowers."
–Ralph Waldo Emerson

WHAT YOU WILL NEED

polymer clay
 1 block ultra blue
 1 block magenta
 1 block pearl
 1 block gold
 1 block violet
 1 block white
 1 block green
 1 block black

Poly Bonder Glue

glass paperweight

wireform diamond mesh
(1/4" [6mm] pattern)

large leaf mold
CLAY COMPANY

1/2" (1cm) flower cutter

texture sheet
GRASS PATTERN BY SHADE-TEX

clay smoothing tool

large ball stylus

release agent

brayer or acrylic rod

clay blade

craft knife

ceramic tile

scissors or metal snips

JUST FOR THE FUN OF IT...
cheap thrills

For a true polymer clay addict, there's nothing like a really great dollar store to get your adrenaline flowing and your imagination soaring. There are always interesting things to cover with clay, so many wonderful things you can turn into tools, items to mold and things to use for patterns and baking forms. When I found these paperweights, I bought a few and put them on my supply shelf where they sat patiently for two years waiting for just the right project. So don't pass up the opportunity to acquire what you know will one day become a potential treasure, especially when it only costs a buck!

ONE
Cover paperweight with clay

Roll a sheet of clay in a color that complements the hydrangea petals through the pasta machine at a no. 5 setting. Cover the paperweight with the sheet of clay. The flower petals and leaves will entirely cover all but the bottom of the paperweight, so don't worry about getting this sheet perfectly smooth. Just take care not to trap any large air bubbles. Use a texture sheet to texture the bottom of the paperweight.

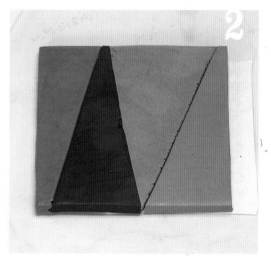

TWO
Create four-part Skinner blend sheet

Cut four triangles composed of two no. 1 layers of clay using hydrangea colors, like pale blue, blue-violet, lavender and pink. These triangles, arranged in a rectangular shape, will be the basis for a four-part Skinner blend sheet. Roll a sheet of pearl clay through the pasta machine at a no. 5 setting and place it underneath the triangles to give a slight pearl tint to the entire blend. Make a Skinner blend sheet (see Basic Techniques, page 14).

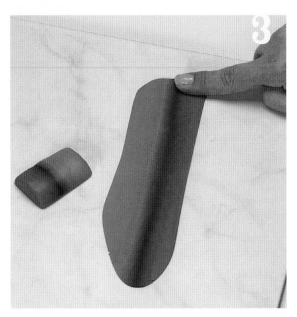

THREE
Create Skinner blend plug

Roll the Skinner blend sheet into a cane, and then compress it into a Skinner blend plug (see Basic Techniques, page 16). Stand the plug on one end and cut off a slice about $1/2$" (1cm) thick. Place the slice on the pasta machine with all of the colors touching the rollers and thin it to a no. 4 setting.

FOUR
Apply petals to paperweight

Burnish the hydrangea-colored sheet of clay to a ceramic tile with your finger. Use the flower cutter to cut out as many petals as you can. You may have to cut several slices from the Skinner blend plug to punch out enough petals to cover the paperweight. Adhere the petals to the paperweight by placing them on the clay-covered surface and then pressing down in the center of each petal with the ball stylus. Continue to adhere the petals until the top and the sides of the paperweight are covered. Bake the paperweight at 275°F for 30 minutes. Let it cool.

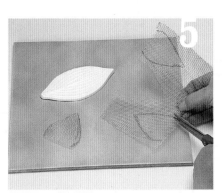

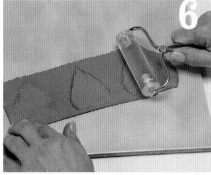

FIVE
Cut out wire mesh for leaves

Determine how large your leaves need to be and use the scissors to cut out three leaf shapes from the diamond mesh. The shapes should be a little narrower and shorter than the actual size of the leaves.

SIX
Adhere mesh to leaf clay

Mix two parts green, one part gold and a pinch of black clay to create the green color used in the leaves. Roll the clay through the pasta machine at a no. 5 setting. Place the mesh leaf shapes on top of the clay and roll over them with a brayer to embed them slightly into the clay.

SEVEN
Cover mesh layer with clay

Cut the leaves apart, making sure not to cut too close to the mesh. Cover each section with another piece of green clay rolled through the pasta machine at a no. 4 setting. Brayer over the top of the layered clay to adhere everything together.

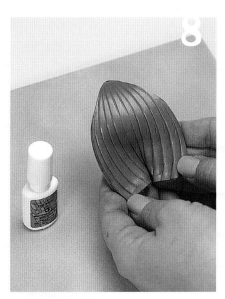

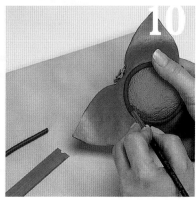

EIGHT
Mold leaves

Spray a little release agent on the green clay and press it firmly into the leaf mold. Remove the clay from the mold and cut away the excess clay with the craft knife so that the leaves will fit around the paperweight. Repeat for two more leaves. Gently bend the leaves into a shape that's pleasing to you and brush a little of the Poly Bonder Glue around the bottom edge of the paperweight.

NINE
Adhere leaves to paperweight

Press the leaves into place around the bottom of the paperweight. The layer of mesh will help them to keep their shape during the baking process.

TEN
Add trim to bottom

Roll a snake of blue-violet clay to about 1/3" (8mm) in diameter. Brush a little glue around the bottom edge of the paperweight and press the snake into place around the bottom edge. Use a clay smoother to blend the seam.

ELEVEN
Apply more petals around bottom

Add a few more flower petals around the bottom of the paperweight between each leaf. Bake the paperweight at 275°F for 30 minutes. Let it cool.

VARIATION **Hydrangea Wastebasket**

This is a small metal wastebasket that was made using the hydrangea technique as a decorative element. The clay was adhered to the metal with glue and then baked on the wastebasket.

GLITZY TILE CLOCK

I had so much fun developing this surface technique. The vibrant colors of the alcohol inks and the gorgeous sheen of the gold pearl powder are almost magical when they're combined to create these wonderful mosaic tiles. Look around for other surfaces you can transform with polymer clay mosaics, such as a small tabletop or box lid. Mosaic tiles made with polymer clay are much easier to cut and shape than traditional ceramic tiles, and you can always custom mix your own colors to create tiles that perfectly match your décor. Don't waste another minute. *Tempus fugit!*

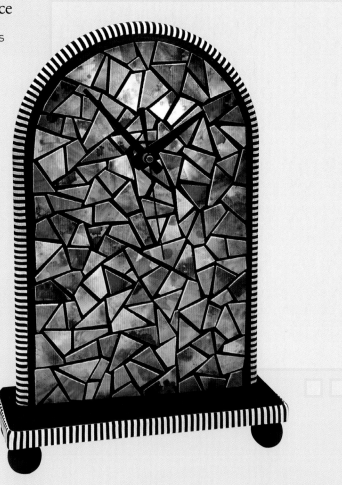

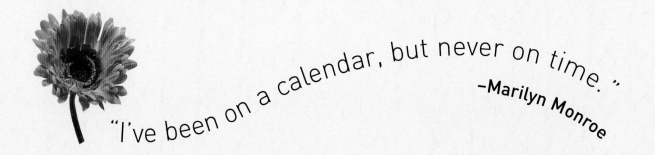

"I've been on a calendar, but never on time."
—Marilyn Monroe

WHAT YOU WILL NEED

polymer clay
   1 block white
   1 block black

liquid polymer clay

wooden arch clock
WALNUT HOLLOW

3/4" (2cm) clock
movement

clock hands

alcohol inks NATURE'S WALK
SET BY RANGER

gold pearl powder

black acrylic paint

rotary cutter with
straight edge

cutting mat

metal ruler

angled clay lift tool

disposable foam brush

craft foam cut into 1"
(3cm) squares

rubbing alcohol

fluffy cosmetic brush

white glue

clay blade

craft knife

ceramic tile

60-grit sandpaper

paintbrush

Before I began this book, I have to admit that I hadn't experimented much with all the powders, inks, paints and other wonderful items that are available to combine with polymer clay. I bought them though, always hoping someday I'd have the opportunity to play around and experiment with all the possibilities they offered.

When I started designing projects for the book, I realized there would never be a better time than this and I couldn't get my hands on those alcohol inks fast enough. I'd seen Tim Holtz do some fantastic things with inks on paper, and I was hoping they'd be just as wonderful combined with clay. I wasn't disappointed, and you won't be either. These colors are unbelievable—and even more amazing in person. I couldn't resist sprinkling on the gold powder and I love the amazing sheen it creates without covering up the vibrancy of the inks. If you're waiting for the perfect time to play around with all those cool products you've been accumulating, there really is no time like the present!

ONE
Coat clock with glue

Use the foam brush to apply a coat of white glue to the front, sides and base of the clock. You'll want to apply the glue anywhere you plan to put clay. Let the glue dry until it's clear.

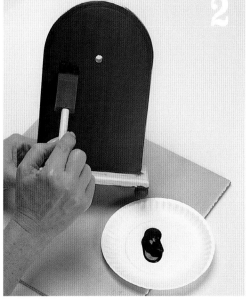

TWO
Paint clock black

Paint the back, bottom and feet of the clock with the black acrylic paint.

THREE
Apply alcohol inks to white clay

Roll a 6" x 6" (15cm x 15cm) piece of white clay on the no. 6 setting on the pasta machine and place it on the ceramic tile. Be sure that the clay is adhered to the tile as smoothly as possible (with no air bubbles). Begin applying drops of the alcohol inks onto the white clay. Use the craft foam squares to help blend the colors together. Work in small sections at a time.

FOUR
Apply gold pearl powder

Use the angled clay lift tool to scoop spoonfuls of the gold pearl powder and sprinkle it over each section.

FIVE
Apply alcohol to clay

Occasionally use the lift tool to apply tiny spoonfuls of alcohol to make the inks bleed into each other. Completely cover the white clay with the inks, powder and alcohol. Let the ink dry, and then use a fluffy brush to brush away the excess gold powder. Bake the clay at 275°F for 30 minutes. Let the clay cool.

SIX
Cut clay into strips

Remove the baked clay from the ceramic tile, and place it on the cutting mat. Use the metal ruler and the rotary cutter to cut the clay into ³/₄" (2cm) strips.

SEVEN
Cut strips into pieces

Cut each strip into ³/₄" (2cm) squares and cut each square into 3 pieces of varying size and shape.

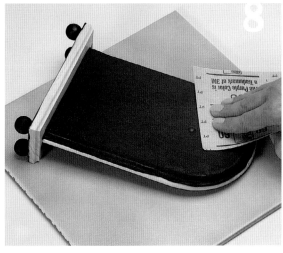

EIGHT
Cover clock front with black clay

Cover the base and the front of the clock with a sheet of black clay rolled to a no. 4 setting on the pasta machine. Trim away the excess black clay from the edges of the clock base with a craft knife or a clay blade. You'll be adding clay to the edges in a later step. Use sandpaper to texture the front and base of the clock.

NINE
Cut hole for clock movement

Use the clay blade to cut out the hole where the clock movement will go. Bake the clock at 275°F for 20 minutes. Let the clock cool.

TEN
Adhere tiles to clock

Use a soft brush to apply a thin layer of liquid clay over the front of the clock. Begin placing your tiles on the clock, making sure the colors are spread out evenly. Leave a 1/4" (6mm) area around the hole uncovered. Press gently to make sure the tiles are adhered. Bake the clock at 275°F for 30 minutes. Let it cool.

ELEVEN
Create striped border

Make a sheet of black and white striped clay (see Basic Techniques, page 19) or use one leftover from another project. Roll the sheet to a no. 5 setting on the pasta machine. Brush a little liquid clay onto the edges of the clock and begin cutting strips from the striped sheet that are wide enough to cover the edges of the clock. Bake at 275°F for 30 minutes. Let the clock cool.

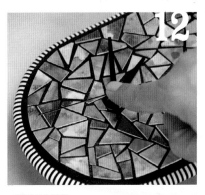

TWELVE
Add clock mechanism

Install the clock movement and the clock hands according to the manufacturer's instructions.

EXTRAORDINARY HOME DÉCOR

After you've worked with polymer clay for just a short amount of time, I promise you'll begin to look at the things around you a little differently. You'll notice an ordinary picture frame that seemed perfectly acceptable just a short time ago and wonder why it suddenly seems so dull and boring.

Then, you'll realize that polymer clay has given you the capability to save that frame and others like it from a lifetime of mediocrity. Turning the ordinary into the extraordinary, you've become a polymer clay superhero!

You'll find lots of things in this section to inspire you. There's a fantasy flower in a wall pocket made entirely of polymer clay, but with the look and feel of leather. There's a fun, funky mirror that's guaranteed to make you smile and, of course, a fabulous colorful picture frame that's anything but ordinary.

89

ART DOLL WITH ATTITUDE

Unusual fabric art dolls have always intrigued me.

I was looking for a way to adapt these dolls into a clay form and woke up in the middle of the night to sketch out a doll I'd dreamed about. I've been making different versions of them for several years now. Although the basic construction has never changed, I've found that each doll has a personality of her own. Use your imagination and have fun creating your own version of these funky dolls.

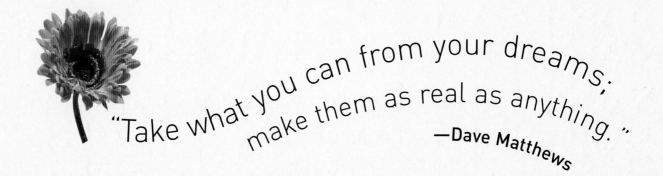

"Take what you can from your dreams; make them as real as anything."
—Dave Matthews

WHAT YOU WILL NEED

polymer clay
- 1 block white
- 1 block beige flesh
- 1 block violet
- 2 blocks black

liquid polymer clay

Poly Bonder Glue

pearl powders RANGER
- sparkle raspberry
- kiwi
- forever violet
- gold
- forever blue
- turquoise
- sparkle true blue

16 large gold jump rings

4 gold beads or charms

plastic-coated 22- and 24-gauge wire

sun face mold AMACO

alphabet tiles rubber stamp STAMP BURN

molding mats CLEARSNAP

pastel decorating chalks

oak gel stain

bamboo skewer

wire cutters

jewelry pliers

needle tool

clay blade

craft knife

soft brush or cosmetic applicators

release agent

index cards

paper towels

JUST FOR THE FUN OF IT...
wired

Plastic-coated wire, such as Fun Wire, can be safely baked with polymer clay and will actually bond with the clay during the baking process if it's firmly attached. It's available in a wide variety of colors and gauges. Using jewelry pliers, you can twist it into any shape you desire.

ONE
Create leaf cane for hair

Using white and violet clays, make a Skinner blend bull's eye cane (see Basic Techniques, page 15). Stand the cane face up on your work surface and use the clay blade to cut straight down the center of the cane. Next, make a black and white striped stack (see Basic Techniques, page 19). Cut off a slice about 1/8" (3mm) thick and insert it between the two halves of the bull's eye cane. Trim it to fit if necessary. Reduce the cane to approximately 1/4" (6mm) in diameter, and pinch it into a leaf shape. Cut about ten thick slices from the leaf cane for the doll's hair.

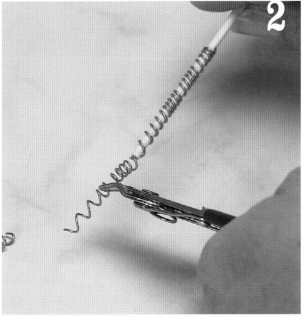

TWO
Curl wire for hair

Use the wire cutters to cut a 15" (38cm) length of 24-gauge plastic-coated wire. Curl the wire around a bamboo skewer to coil it. Remove the wire and cut it into ten equal pieces.

91

THREE
Insert wire into leaf cane slices to create hair

Insert one end of each wire piece into one slice of the leaf cane. Bake with the wires in place at 275°F for 30 minutes. Let them cool.

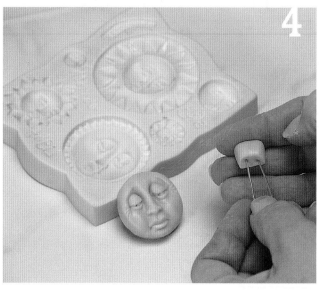

FOUR
Create face and neck

Apply a release agent to a ball of beige flesh clay and insert it into the sun face mold. Trim around the face with the craft knife and smooth away any rough edges. To create the neck, form a small ball of beige flesh clay into a neck shape. Cut a 3" (8cm) piece of 22-gauge wire and bend it in half. Insert the ends through the top of the neck leaving a 1/2" (1cm) loop at the top.

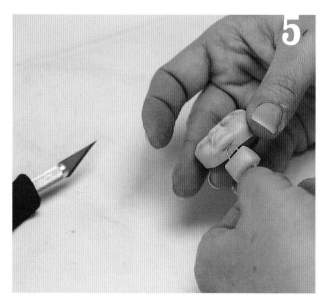

FIVE
Connect head and neck

Use your craft knife to make a small slit in the bottom of the face where the neck should go. Push the wire loop into this slit and press gently to adhere the face and the neck.

SIX
Add color to face and add hair

Insert the baked leaf pieces around the top of the head. Use a soft brush to apply the decorating chalks, giving the face a little color. Bake the face on an index card at 275°F for 30 minutes. Let it cool.

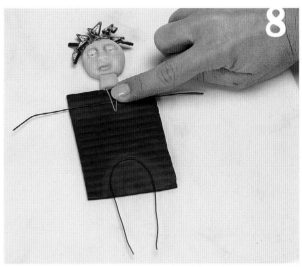

SEVEN
Create body

Cut two 4" x 2³/₄" (10cm x 7cm) rectangles from the black clay rolled through the pasta machine at the thickest setting. Texture one side of one rectangle with a molding mat and turn it textured side down onto an index card. Cut a 7" (18cm) piece of black 24-gauge plastic-coated wire and bend it into a "U" shape. Place it near the bottom of the rectangle to anchor the legs. Lightly press the wire into the clay. Add another 7" (18cm) length of wire for the arms, pressing it across the top of the clay at the level where the arms will be connected.

EIGHT
Connect head and neck to body

Place the baked head and neck in place and press the protruding wires gently into the black clay of the body.

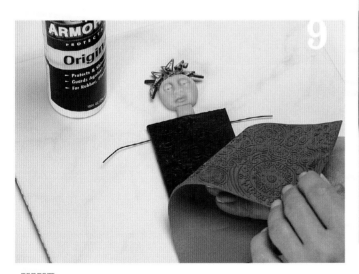

NINE
Complete body and texture

Lay the second rectangle of black clay over the first and smooth the edges together. Apply a release agent to the black clay and press the molding mat evenly into the clay. Press fairly hard to adhere the two pieces together and embed the wires. Achieving a good impression in the clay will also help the pearl powder effects to show up.

TEN
Apply pearl powders

Using your fingers or a soft brush, apply the pearl powders over the black clay to bring out the stamped design.

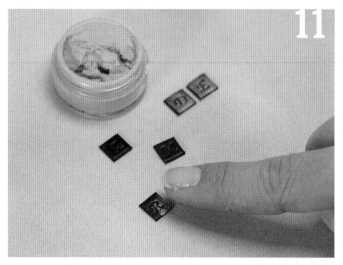

ELEVEN
Create phrase

Roll a piece of black clay through the pasta machine at a no. 4 setting. Apply a release agent to the clay and then impress it with the alphabet stamp. Use a clay blade to cut out the word "DREAM." Using your fingers or a paintbrush, highlight the letters with the gold pearl powder. Bake at 275°F for 30 minutes. Let it cool.

TWELVE
Adhere word to body

Apply the letters to the doll's torso with a drop of the liquid clay. Bake the doll on the index card at 275°F for 30 minutes. Let it cool.

THIRTEEN
Create segments for arms and legs

Roll a sheet of black clay through the pasta machine at a no. 3 setting. Spray a release agent on the clay and use the molding mat to texture it. You can make all of your tiles the same by using the same small section of the molding mat over and over. You'll need to make six tiles for the legs that are about ³/₄" x 1¹/₄" (2cm x 3cm). The six arm tiles should be ¹/₂" x 1" (1cm x 3cm) each. Apply pearl powders to the pieces and use the needle tool to make small holes near the top and bottom of each piece for the jump rings. Bake the tiles on an index card at 275°F for 30 minutes. Let them cool.

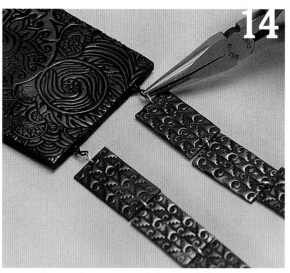

FOURTEEN
Attach arms and legs

Use jewelry pliers to form the ends of the arm and leg wires into loops. Then wrap the ends of the wire around the base of the loops to secure them. Trim any excess wire. Use jewelry pliers to open all of the jump rings and then link three arm pieces together for each arm and three leg pieces together for each leg.

FIFTEEN
Create "hands" and "feet"

Attach beads or charms with jump rings to the last arm and leg segments to serve as hands and feet.

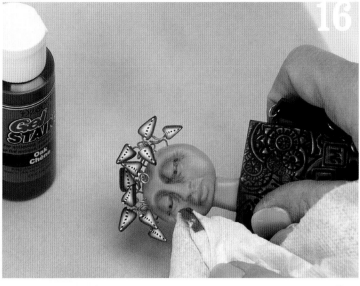

SIXTEEN
Color face and neck with stain

Use a paintbrush to apply a coat of oak gel stain to the doll's face and neck. Wipe off the excess with a paper towel.

SEVENTEEN
Create wire hanger

Make a wire loop from the 22-gauge wire for hanging your doll. Brush a little glue in the center of the doll's body right below the neck. Press the wire into place and allow the glue to dry. Add a few drops of liquid clay over the wire and cut a small rectangle of black clay to hide the ends of the wire. Bake again at 275°F for 30 minutes. Let it cool.

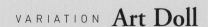

VARIATION **Art Doll**

A girl's gotta have friends! Experiment with different types of hair, arms or legs. Group a few art dolls together and hang them in your studio. Use the alphabet stamp to add an inspiring word or phrase to each one.

FANTASY FLOWER WALL POCKET

Bring the special charm of flowers into your home
with this funky little wall pocket. It will add interest to
any room, and no one will believe it's not made of leather.
The clay used in this project must be both extremely strong and flexible,
so I highly recommend using Kato Polyclay for the best results.

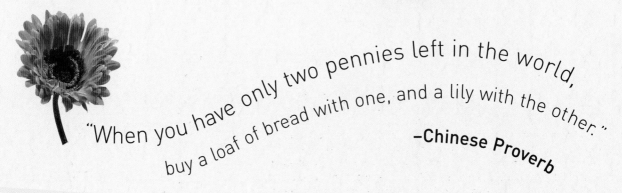

"When you have only two pennies left in the world,
buy a loaf of bread with one, and a lily with the other."
—Chinese Proverb

WHAT YOU WILL NEED

polymer clay
  2 blocks black
  1 block gold
  1 block green
  1 block violet
  1 block magenta
  1 block pearl
  1 block ultra blue

Poly Bonder Glue

wall pocket pattern (at right)

rubber stamp STITCHED QUILL BY STAMPENDOUS!

Mica Magic ink
  green
  purple
  bright blue
  yellow gold

plastic-coated purple wire (24-gauge)

white or light-colored pen

wire cutters

pliers

$1/16$" (2mm) mini circle hand punch

cosmetic sponges

parchment paper

clay blade

craft knife

ceramic tile

polyester batting

60-grit sandpaper

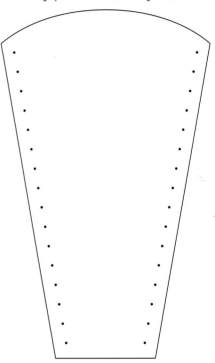

Wall Pocket Pattern Front
Enlarge pattern to 181% to bring to full size.

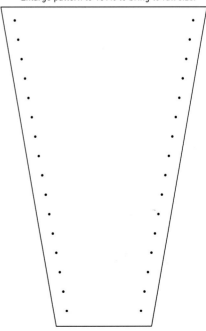

Wall Pocket Pattern Back
Enlarge pattern to 181% to bring to full size.

ONE
Stamp clay with mica ink

Condition two sheets of black clay and roll them each through the pasta machine at a no. 4 setting. Place the sheets on a large ceramic tile (the clay sheets should not overlap) and make sure they're adhered well. Take care not to trap any air bubbles. Lightly texture the surface of the clay using the 60-grit sandpaper. Use the cosmetic sponges to apply the mica inks to the rubber stamp, making sure to apply different colors in different areas of the stamp. Stamp the colors lightly onto the clay. Don't press too hard—you want to transfer the colors, not impress the pattern into the clay.

TWO
Create front and back sections of wall pocket

Use the patterns provided to create templates for cutting the front and back sections of the wall pocket. When creating the template, be sure to mark the hole placement as shown on each of the pattern pieces. Lay the template on top of the clay and cut around it with the clay blade. Bake both pieces on the ceramic tile at 275°F for 30 minutes. Let them cool. Place the templates back on the baked clay and use a light-colored pen to mark the placement of the holes.

THREE
Punch holes for lacing

Finish marking the hole placement using the light-colored pen. Use the 1/16" (2mm) circle punch to create holes in both pieces of the baked clay.

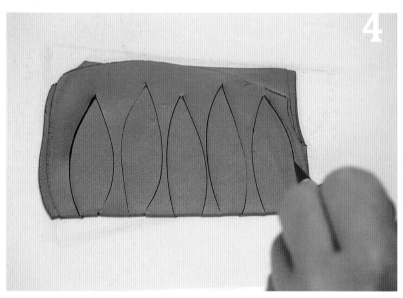

FOUR
Create petals

Mix a little gold clay into a large ball of green clay. Roll the mixture through the pasta machine at a no. 3 setting. Use the craft knife to cut out five free-form petal shapes.

FIVE
Arrange petals together

Pinch one end of each petal and arrange the pinched ends together. Cut a rectangular strip from the green-gold clay and wrap it around the base of the petals to secure the arrangement. Make sure to leave a 1/2" (1cm) opening at the bottom of the petal base where you'll insert the stem of the flower in a later step.

SIX
Add berries

Mix a tiny amount of violet into the magenta clay and roll several little balls from the mixture. Press the balls around the base of the petals. Bake the petal cluster on a piece of polyester batting at 275°F for 30 minutes. Let it cool.

SEVEN
Create blue spiral stem

Mix a little pearl clay into a large ball of ultra blue clay. Roll the mixture into a 16" (41cm) snake about $1/2$" (1cm) in diameter. Taper one end to a point by rolling it on your work surface. Place the snake on a piece of parchment paper and coil the tapered end into a spiral. Bake the coiled clay on the parchment paper at 275°F for 30 minutes. Let it cool.

EIGHT
Lace wall pocket together

Use the wire cutters to cut two 18" (46cm) lengths of purple wire. Line up the two clay pieces and, starting at the top, push the wire through the punched holes from the back to the front. Coil the ends of the wires on the back of the wall pocket using the pliers to secure them. I find it's easier to lace each side a little at a time, switching from the right to the left. As you lace the pieces together, the front piece will flex somewhat to form the pouch for the flower. When both sides are joined together, slide the excess wire back through the laces on the back of the wall pocket to secure them.

NINE
Assemble flower and create wire hanger

Use the craft knife to trim the blue stem as needed so it fits inside the green petals. You may need to trim the opening inside the petal section also. Remove the petals from the stem and insert the straight end of the stem through the bottom of the wall pocket. Brush glue inside the petal opening and insert the straight end of the stem into place. Let the glue dry.

Make a hanger for the wall pocket out of the purple wire and secure it to the existing wire on the back of the wall pocket.

SEUSSICAL FLOWER VASE

SEUSSICAL FLOWER VASE

No one has done more to encourage and inspire the world to read than the amazing Dr. Seuss. His use of color and his wonderful illustrations continue to influence many artists, myself included. I'm sure the whimsical, leaning flowers resting on their improbable black-and-white stems on this vase would grow in abundance in Dr. Seuss's world. I hope you find that it's just the thing to get your creativity flowing. Because it has a glass lining, this vase is fully functional, too. Have fun combining glorious colors and textures and let the clay become your canvas. The possibilities are truly endless—just ask Dr. Seuss.

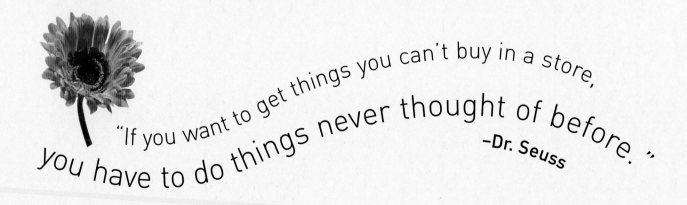

"If you want to get things you can't buy in a store, you have to do things never thought of before."

—Dr. Seuss

WHAT YOU WILL NEED

polymer clay
  2 blocks white
  1 block violet
  1 block ultra blue
  1 block orange
  1 block magenta
  1 block green
  1 block yellow
  1 block black

liquid polymer clay

purchased glass vase
with smooth sides

small leaf-shaped cutter

Marxit tool

acrylic rod

needle tool

clay blade

craft knife

ceramic tile

60- and 20-grit sand-paper

pencil eraser

When you're making a project that's as dimensional as this vase or that's decorated on all sides, it's really difficult to keep things from becoming distorted. No matter how careful you are, you'll have to handle and turn the piece quite a bit, which leads to fingerprints, dents and dings in the clay. Save yourself a lot of grief and bake the piece as many times as necessary for worry-free handling. As long as you're baking at the correct temperature, you can't hurt the clay. I've baked some pieces as many as 25 times and never had a problem. And now that we have that amazing substance liquid polymer clay, it's no problem to adhere unbaked and baked clay together.

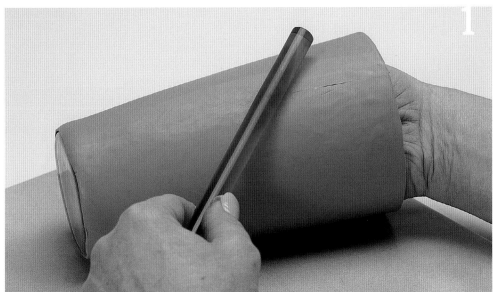

ONE
Cover vase with clay

Prepare the vase by removing any stickers or labels, and by washing it with soap and water. Mix one block of white clay with 1/2 block of violet clay and 1/4 block of ultra blue clay. The amount of clay you need will vary depending on the size of the vase you are covering. Just remember to keep the proportions the same, and mix a little more clay than you think you may need.

   Roll the clay through the pasta machine at a no. 4 setting. (You may have to roll more than one sheet to cover the vase completely.) Begin covering the vase by laying an edge of the clay sheet on the vase and wrapping it tightly around the glass. Smooth the clay as you wrap and press out any air bubbles. Smooth the seams by rubbing over them with your fingers or an acrylic rod.

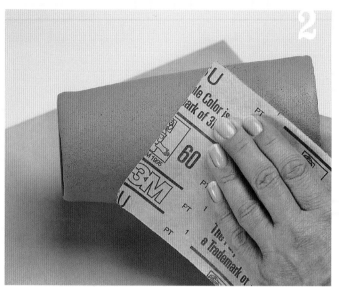

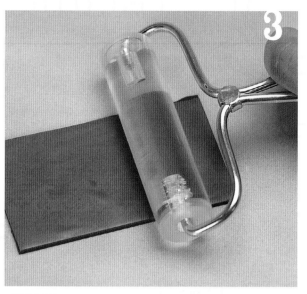

TWO
Texture clay

When the clay is as smooth as you can make it, begin pressing the 60-grit sandpaper over the surface to hide fingerprints, seams and any other imperfections. Then add even more texture by going lightly over the clay with the 20-grit sandpaper. Bake the vase at 275°F for 30 minutes. Let it cool.

THREE
Begin to create flower petals

Condition $1/3$ block each of orange and magenta clay. Run each through the pasta machine at a no. 5 setting. Stack the sheets and run the acrylic rod over them gently to adhere them together.

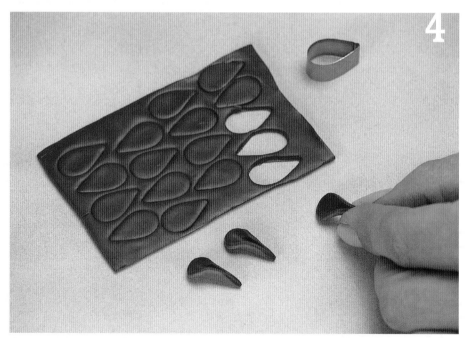

FOUR
Shape petals

Cut out 25 to 30 petals from the orange and magenta stack using the leaf cutter. Use your fingers to pinch the pointed end so that each petal curls up slightly, making both colors visible.

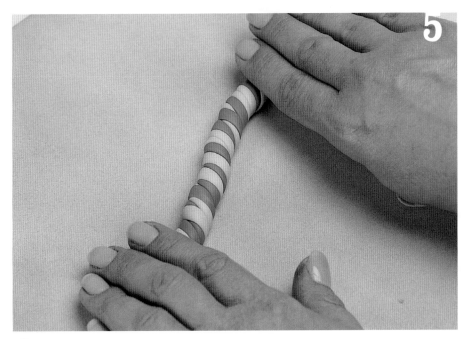

FIVE
Begin to marble green and yellow clay for leaves

Condition 1¼ block each of green and yellow clay. Form each color into a snake. Twist the green and yellow snakes together to begin to marble the clay. Fold the twisted snake in half and continue to twist.

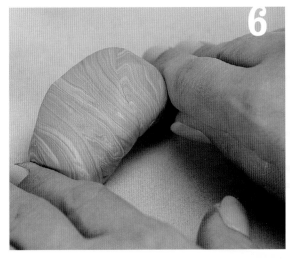

SIX
Finish marbling clay

Continue to twist, roll and fold the green and yellow clay until the two colors are marbled together. Roll the yellow-green clay through the pasta machine at a no. 5 setting. Cut this sheet in half with a clay blade and stack the halves. Use the leaf cutter to cut out 13 to 15 leaves. Pinch the rounded end of each leaf so it curls slightly.

SEVEN
Create black and white striped sheet

Create a striped sheet of clay or use one left over from a previous project (see Basic Techniques, page 19). The striped sheet should be about 4" x 2½" (10cm x 6cm). Roll it through the pasta machine at a no. 7 setting. If you'd like, you can impress the 5mm or 7mm side of the Marxit tool on the striped sheet to help you cut the consistently-sized strips you'll need for the next step.

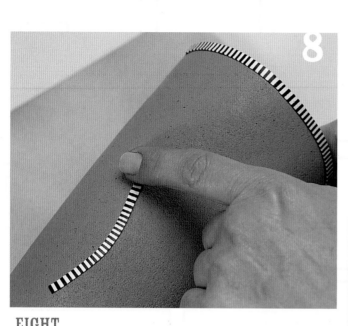

EIGHT
Add border and flower stems to vase

Cut four or five ¹/₄" (6mm) strips from your black and white striped sheet to serve as stems for the flowers. Try varying the length of the stems to add more interest to the vase. Brush a little liquid polymer clay on the back of each one, and space them evenly around the vase, pressing gently to adhere them. Cut a few more ¹/₄" (6mm) strips and adhere them end-to-end around the top of the vase as a border, using liquid polymer clay to adhere them.

NINE
Add petals and leaves

Brush a little liquid clay on the backs of the petals and leaves. Arrange 5 to 6 petals around the top of each striped stem and 2 to 3 leaves along the lengths of the stems, pressing gently to adhere them to the vase.

TEN
Add flower centers

Mix a small amount of violet and ultra blue together and roll approximately 40 tiny balls. Make an indention in each flower center with a pencil eraser and brush a tiny bit of liquid clay into the impression. Place 7 or 8 balls into the center of each flower. Bake the vase again at 275°F for 30 minutes. Let it cool.

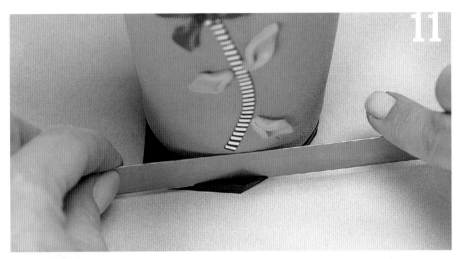

Cut black clay for vase bottom

Condition ¹/₂ block of black clay and run it through the pasta machine at a no. 2 setting. Cut the piece of clay in half with a clay blade and stack one half on top of the other. Spread a little liquid polymer clay evenly over the bottom of the vase and press it firmly into the black clay. Trim the black clay flush with the sides of the vase.

TWELVE
Texture bottom of vase

Use the 60-grit sandpaper to add texture to the black clay. Bake the vase at 275°F for 30 minutes. Let it cool.

**PSST...
HERE'S A TIP**

I like to use black and white stripes and swirls as an accent to the bright colors I use in my work, but you can make stripes in any color combination you like. Try using muted, earthtone colors or a lighter and darker version of the same color for a more subtle effect.

PUT ON A HAPPY FACE (MASK)

PUT ON A HAPPY FACE (MASK)

There may be a limit to how much you can do to change your own face, but creating a face mask is a no-holds-barred adventure into expressions forbidden on the "regular" face. This funky face is made with several Skinner blend canes and some pieces cut from a striped loaf. Although it may look complicated, it's really not. If you're inspired by the power of creating a face from scratch, you can make several variations of these masks and group them together for an eye-catching wall display.

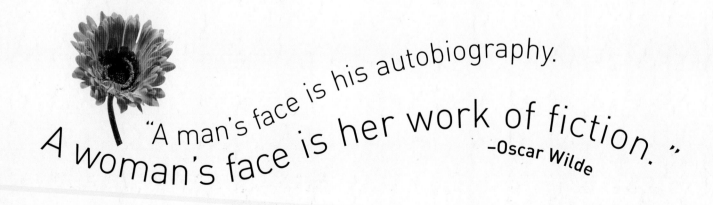

"A man's face is his autobiography. A woman's face is her work of fiction."
—Oscar Wilde

WHAT YOU WILL NEED

polymer clay
   3 blocks black
   1 block white
   1 block green
   1 block yellow
   1 block violet
   1 block turquoise
   1 block orange
   1 block red
   1 block magenta
   1 block ultra blue

liquid polymer clay

mask template (at right)

non-stick form to bake on (large vase or drape mold)

10" (25cm) plastic-coated wire (for hanger)

texture sheet SWIRLED DOTS PATTERN BY SHADE-TEX

1/8" (3mm) circle pattern cutter

brayer or acrylic rod

clay blade

craft knife

Mask Pattern

Enlarge pattern to 181% to bring to full size.

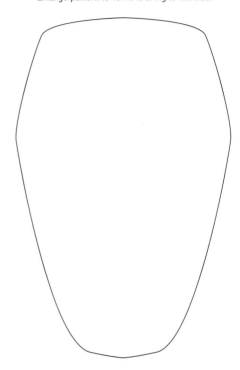

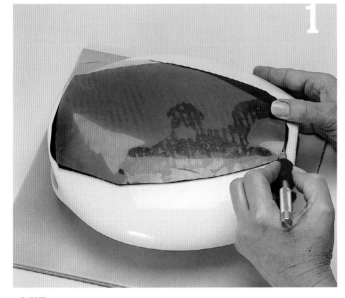

ONE
Prepare black clay and cut around template

Condition two packages of black clay at a no. 1 setting on the pasta machine. Place the sheet of clay on your baking form and place the template on the clay. Use a craft knife to cut out the face shape, and discard the excess clay.

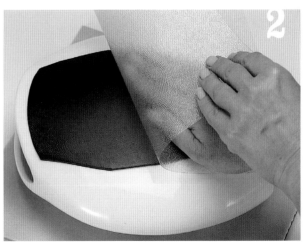

TWO
Texture face

With the clay still on the baking form, lightly texture the face shape with the texture sheet. Lay the template back on top of the textured clay and trim away any distortion. Do not remove the clay from the baking form—you'll be decorating and baking the mask on the form.

THREE
Make different Skinner blend bull's eye canes

Make several Skinner blend bull's eye canes (see Basic Techniques, page 15). I used the following combinations: black to white, green to yellow, violet to light blue, turquoise to white, violet to turquoise, magenta to orange, and red to light pink. You'll also need to make a black and white striped stack and a black and white striped sheet (see Basic Techniques, pages 18 and 19).

FOUR
Create hair

Reduce the black to white bull's eye cane to about 1/2" (1cm) in diameter. Flatten one end. Run the flattened end through the pasta machine at a no. 1 setting. Trim the ends of the cane, cut it in half and stack one half on top of the other. Repeat the cutting and stacking three more times. Reduce the cane to the desired size and pinch it into a triangle shape. Cut several thin slices for the hair, and arrange them across the top of the face. Reduce the green to yellow Skinner blend bull's eye cane to about 1/4" (6mm) in diameter. Cut thin slices of the cane and place them between the black and white triangle.

FIVE
Create eyes

The eyes are made from slices of the turquoise to white bull's eye cane. The eyelids are made in the same way as the hair. You can make the lines very fine by cutting the triangle in half and recombining it. Reduce the recombined cane, cut it in half one more time, and push the bottom of the triangles together. Flatten one long side against your work surface to get the desired shape. Cut two thick slices to serve as the eyelids. Roll a piece of black clay through the pasta machine at a no. 6 setting and use the 1/8" (3mm) circle punch to make the pupils.

SIX
Create nose

Roll a piece of black clay into a log about 1/3" (8mm) in diameter. Taper one end so you have what looks like a long, pointed stick. Begin coiling the log from the pointed end until you get the shape you would like for the nose. Use a clay blade to cut a slice from the black and white striped sheet. Arrange it on top of the coiled nose shape.

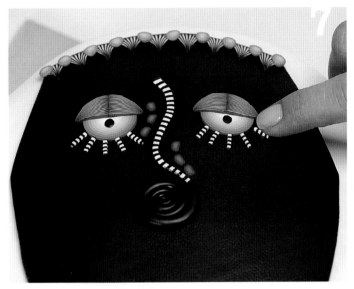

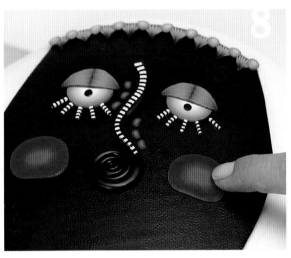

SEVEN
Create eyelashes

Cut a thin slice of the black and white stack and divide it into small sections to make the eyelashes. Reduce a piece of the violet to turquoise bull's eye cane to 1/4" (6mm) in diameter. Cut six thin slices and arrange them around the nose.

EIGHT
Create cheeks

Cut two thick slices from the magenta to orange Skinner blend bull's eye cane. Use your brayer or knitting needle to flatten them until they are in proportion with the size of the face.

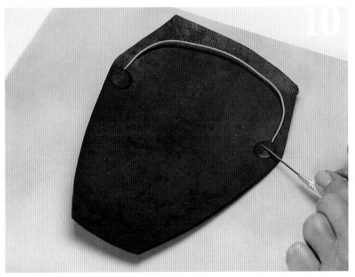

NINE
Create mouth

Cut a piece from the black and white striped sheet to make the teeth. The lips are made from a red to light pink Skinner blend bull's eye cane which is pinched into a triangle shape, cut in half, and recombined by placing the bottom of the triangles together. Cut two thick slices and alter them by pinching and stretching the points until you get the shape you want for the lips. Cut a small section of the green to yellow bull's eye cane, flatten one end, and run it through the pasta machine at a no. 1 setting. Cut three thin slices and arrange them under the mouth. Bake the mask at 275°F for 30 minutes and let it cool completely on the form.

TEN
Create hanger for mask

Gently lift the mask off of the form. Cut a piece of plastic-coated wire and curl the ends into circles. Put a couple of drops of liquid polymer clay on either side of the back of the mask. Set the wire in place and add a small ball of black clay on top of the wire. Gently flatten the clay to make sure it's adhered to the wire. Place the face back on the form and bake it at 275°F for 30 minutes. Let the mask cool completely on the form.

HELLO GORGEOUS
MIRROR

HELLO GORGEOUS MIRROR

Mirror, mirror on the wall…even if you're not looking your best, this fun and whimsical mirror will always tell you what you want to hear—or at least it will make you smile! A set of alphabet cutters, some face molds and a few simple cane slices turn a plain mirror into one that's fit for a queen.

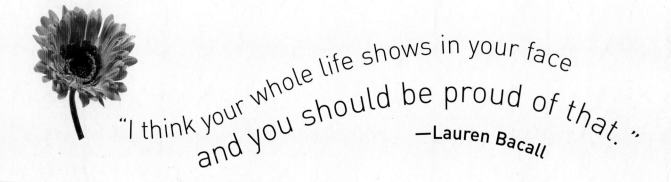

"I think your whole life shows in your face and you should be proud of that."
—Lauren Bacall

WHAT YOU WILL NEED

polymer clay

  3 blocks black
  1 block yellow
  1 block magenta
  1 block silver
  1 block white
  1 block pearl
  1 block green

liquid polymer clay

Poly Bonder Glue

6" (15cm) round craft store mirror

24-gauge plastic-coated wire BLACK AND WHITE

2 grommets

polymer clay molds SUN, MOON AND TRIBAL BY AMACO

pastel decorating chalks

alphabet cutters

texture sheet LINEN PATTERN BY SHADE-TEX

wire cutters

small clamp

hand drill

angled clay lift tool

bowl with 7½" (19cm) diameter

soft brush or cotton swabs

parchment paper

release agent

needle tool

clay blade

wavy blade

craft knife

ONE
Join two pieces of clay for back of mirror

Roll out two pieces of black clay at a no. 1 setting on the pasta machine. Lay them side by side on a piece of parchment paper and smooth the seams together by rubbing them with your fingers to make one continuous piece of clay. Then adhere the two pieces further by smoothing over the seam with the angled clay lift tool.

TWO
Cut out circle

Use a bowl with a 7½" (19cm) diameter as a template for cutting out the circle for the back of the mirror. Lay the bowl on the large sheet of black clay and cut around the rim with a craft knife. Remove the excess clay.

THREE
Texture clay circle

Spray a little release agent on the clay and then lay the texture sheet on the clay circle. Texture the sheet well, especially along the seam. If the circle becomes distorted after it is textured, simply place the bowl back on the circle and trim away any excess clay with a craft knife. Lay another piece of parchment paper over the clay and use it to help you flip the circle over. Remove the first sheet of parchment paper from the clay circle. The textured side of the circle will become the back of the mirror.

FOUR
Create border for mirror

Roll a second piece of black clay through the pasta machine at a no. 2 setting. Center the mirror on the clay and cut around it with a craft knife. Lift the mirror off of the clay and discard the circle cutout.

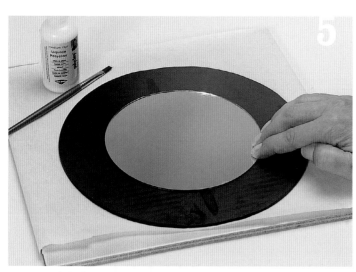

FIVE
Adhere mirror to clay backing

Apply liquid clay to the back of the mirror and center it on the clay circle you made in step 3. Press the mirror gently into the clay to adhere it.

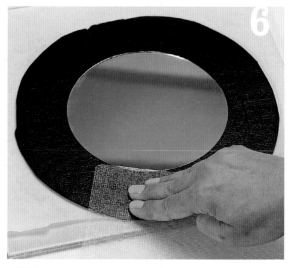

SIX
Add border around mirror and re-texture

Place the sheet of black clay from step 4 on top of the clay circle, carefully lining up the mirror and the cut-out circle in the black clay sheet. Press gently to adhere the black clay pieces together. Place the metal bowl on top of the black frame and line up the rim of the bowl with the clay circle beneath the black sheet. Trim around the bowl with the craft knife. Texture the frame well to adhere the black circles together. Place the bowl back on top of the frame and trim away any of the distortion from the texturing process.

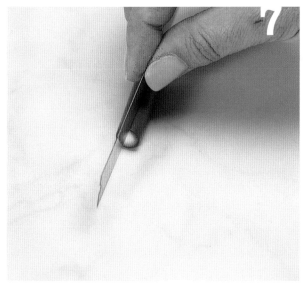

SEVEN
Make Skinner blend bull's eye cane for border

Make a magenta to white Skinner blend bull's eye cane (see Basic Techniques, page 15). Reduce the cane to 1/2" (1cm) in diameter. Cut off a 2" (5cm) section of the cane and lay it on your work surface. Center the clay blade over the cane section and cut straight down the length of the cane. You should now have two canes that are half circles.

EIGHT
Apply cane slices to mirror frame

Run a thin line of liquid clay around the rim of the mirror. Cut thin slices from the half bull's eye canes and apply them around the edge of the mirror.

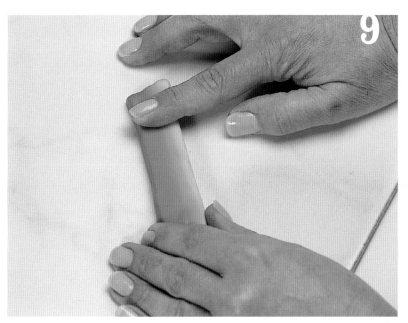

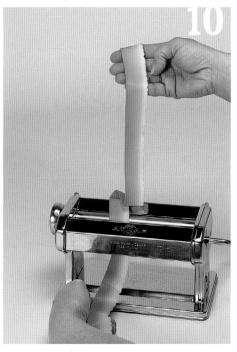

NINE
Make Skinner blend plug for letters

Make a green to yellow Skinner blend plug (see Basic Techniques, page 16). Lay the plug flat on your work surface so that the colors are running vertically. Using your fingers and the palm of your hand, flatten, thin and lengthen the plug, keeping the colors running vertically.

TEN
Thin out Skinner blend plug

With both colors touching the rollers, run the green and yellow sheet of clay through the pasta machine at the thickest setting. Continue to roll the blend through the pasta machine at progressively thinner settings until you reach the no. 4 setting. The ribbon of clay will be long and narrow.

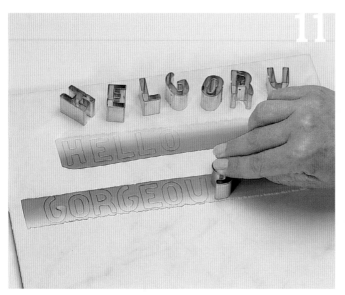

ELEVEN
Punch out letters

Lay the lengthened blend on your work surface and use the alphabet cutters to punch out the phrase "HELLO GORGEOUS." Arrange the letters in place around the mirror.

TWELVE
Add decorative striped pieces around letters

Make a striped sheet of clay (see Basic Techniques, page 19), or use a leftover sheet from another project. Run the sheet through the pasta machine on progressively thinner settings until you get to the no. 6 setting. Cut thin strips from the sheet and apply them around the letters.

Use a needle tool to mark where the grommets should be placed (refer to the picture of finished mirror on page 110). Enlarge the holes slightly and insert the grommets into the clay. Bake the mirror at 275°F for 30 minutes. Let it cool.

THIRTEEN
Create faces

Mix a small amount of silver into the pearl clay. Spray the clay with the release agent and make four different faces from the molds.

FOURTEEN
Embellish faces and add to mirror frame

Use a soft brush or a cotton swab to apply the decorating chalks to the faces, and add a few simple cane slices for hair. Apply a little liquid clay to the backs of the faces and place them around the mirror frame.

FIFTEEN
Add accent pieces

Use the wavy blade to cut thin strips of clay from the leftover Skinner blend plug you made for the Fashion Fold Earrings (see page 37) and adhere them with liquid polymer clay. Make a simple cane, such as a jelly roll (see Basic Techniques, page 18), and add a few slices from the cane to fill in any empty spaces around the mirror. Bake the mirror at 275°F for 30 minutes. Let it cool.

SIXTEEN
Remove and attach grommets

Gently pull out the grommets from the mirror and use the needle tool to poke out the small chunks of baked clay left inside. Brush glue on the grommets and insert them back into the holes. Let the glue dry.

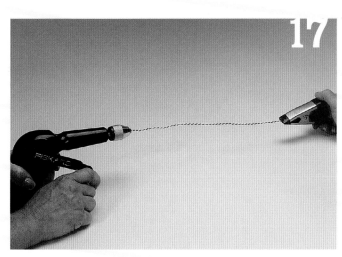

SEVENTEEN
Create wire hanger

Use the wire cutters to cut a 2' (61cm) section of the black and white wires. Twist the ends together slightly. Anchor one end to a table with the clamp (or have a friend hold the clamp) and insert the other end into the hand drill. Use the hand drill to tightly twist the wires together.

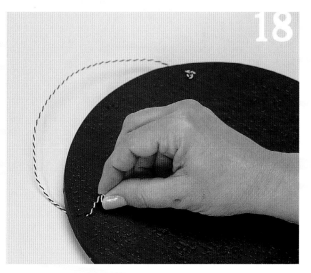

EIGHTEEN
Attach wire hanger to mirror

Insert the wire through the grommets on the mirror frame. Coil the ends of the wire on the back of the mirror to secure them in place.

FREEFORM PHOTO FRAME

FREEFORM PHOTO FRAME

Anyone who has children knows that life isn't always smiles, hugs and a day at the beach. But these perfect moments are the ones we remember as our children grow up faster than we could ever have imagined.

Your favorite snapshots deserve to be displayed in a fabulous frame, and nothing could be more special than one you've made yourself. This frame is a riot of color and texture that features all of the basic canes shown in this book applied in a freeform way to a canvas of black clay. It's the perfect way to showcase that perfect moment you'll never forget.

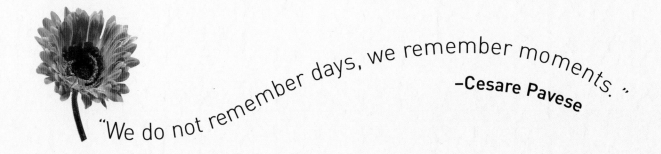

"We do not remember days, we remember moments."

–Cesare Pavese

WHAT YOU WILL NEED

polymer clay
   1 block black
   1 block white

any bright clay colors of
your choice

liquid polymer clay

wooden picture frame

white PVA-type glue

clay-smoothing tool

disposable foam brush

paintbrush

clay blade

craft knife

ceramic tile

snap it up

Originally, this project was not meant to be part of the book. It was actually a companion piece I made to go along with a bracelet project I taped for the Carol Duvall Show. But, as the book began to take shape, I thought this frame would be a great way to bring all of the basic caning techniques together into one project. Although there's nothing complicated about any of the canes, the impact comes from using so many different sizes, shapes and colors together on the black background. The trick is to keep the cane patterns themselves as simple as possible so they don't compete with each other—or with the snapshot you choose to show off in the frame.

ONE
Coat frame with glue

You can't always be sure how wood will react in the oven, so before you begin the project I recommend that you bake your frame at 275°F for 30 minutes to make sure the frame doesn't warp or fall apart in the heat. Once the frame has cooled, use the disposable foam brush to apply a coat of white glue to the front and sides of the frame. Let the glue dry until it is clear and tacky.

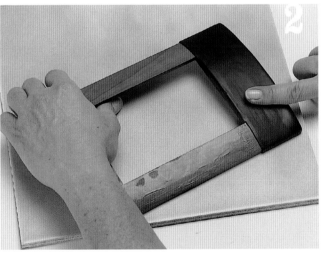

TWO
Cover frame with black clay

Roll the black clay through the pasta machine at a no. 4 setting. Cover the picture frame in sections, taking care to smooth the seams and eliminate any air bubbles. Trim away any excess clay with the clay blade.

THREE
Smooth seams

Use a clay-smoothing tool to blend any remaining seams together. Bake the frame at 275°F for 30 minutes. Let the frame cool gradually in the oven to minimize the chance of cracks forming in the clay due to the expansion of the wood.

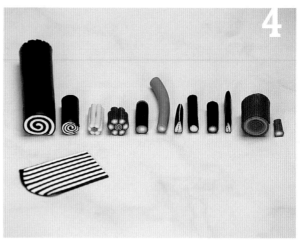

FOUR
Create canes and embellishments

Construct a black and white jelly roll cane and a black and white striped sheet. Also construct several Skinner blend bull's eye canes (see Basic Techniques, pages 14–19) and leaf canes in various colors (see Art Doll project, page 91).

FIVE
Create center for flower cane

You can create flower canes in any color combination that you like. For this cane, I used a green snake wrapped in two shades of purple clay for the flower center. Begin by rolling a lime green snake to 1/2" (1cm) diameter. Roll a sheet of violet clay to a no. 6 setting on the pasta machine, and a sheet of lavender clay to a no. 4 setting. Wrap the green snake in the violet clay, and then wrap the lavender clay around both.

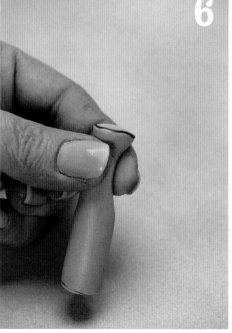

SIX
Reduce center of flower cane

Reduce the green and purple cane to 1/4" (6mm) by first "choking" the cane on both ends and then rolling it on your work surface to smooth it.

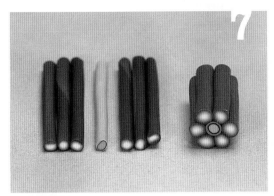

SEVEN
Assemble flower cane

Create a violet to white Skinner blend bull's eye cane (see Basic Techniques, page 15) and reduce it to 1/4" (6mm) in diameter. Cut the cane into six equal sections and adhere them around the center cane. Press all of the individual canes together lightly with your fingers to adhere them.

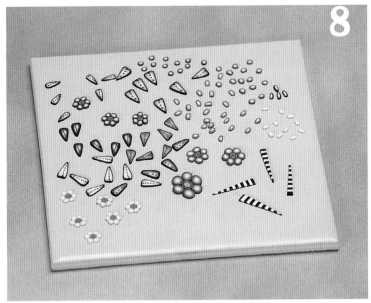

EIGHT
Cut cane slices

Gather all of your different canes and striped sheets together and begin cutting thin slices and laying them on a ceramic tile in preparation for applying them to your frame. Because you're using so many different elements in this project, it's best to stick to canes with simple designs.

NINE
Apply cane slices to frame

Use a paintbrush to apply a thin layer of liquid polymer clay to the black clay base. Begin placing your cane slices onto the frame, working one small section at a time. Apply the slices in a freeform way, varying the colors, sizes and cane styles. When you're happy with the placement of the cane slices, press gently to adhere them to the frame. Bake the frame at 275°F for 30 minutes. Let the frame cool in the oven.

GALLERY

As you've seen by now, polymer clay has amazing potential and versatility. Here's a small sampling of work from just a few of the talented artists working in polymer clay today, including some of my own pieces.

Snail Woman
by Lesley Polinko

The unlikely combination of a beautifully sculpted face and a real snail shell bring to mind a magical fairyland in this unique and delicate piece.

Frog Boy on a Mushroom
by Lesley Polinko

Artist Lesley Polinko has an amazing eye for detail and a wonderful ability to bring these enchanting and magical sculptures to life.

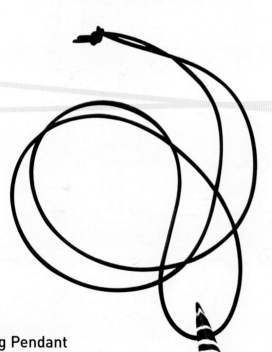

Arrowhead Moon
by Leslie Blackford

This chubby-cheeked man in the moon was formed and sculpted over an arrowhead artifact from the artist's own collection.

Pig Pendant
by Leslie Blackford

This charming little pig pendant is a perfect representation of Leslie Blackford's engaging sculptural style.

Loud Whispers
by Sue Kelsey and Leigh Ross

The wonderful layered textures and colors of Sue Kelsey's polymer clay beads are beautifully enhanced by Leigh Ross' exquisite silverwork.

Stamped Skinner Blend Bookmarks
by Cathy Johnston

Cathy Johnston's elegant stamped bookmarks are so incredibly soft and flexible, it's hard to believe they're made of polymer clay and not leather.

Asparagus Picture Frame
by Kim Cavender

This textured frame is a tribute to my favorite vegetable. Thin cane slices were applied to the asparagus stalks for a realistic touch.

Eggcentric
by Dawn Schiller

Dawn Schiller's fun and whimsical sculptures, known as Eggcentrics, have wonderful expression and character that reflect the artist's sense of humor.

Stone Flower & Butterfly Pendant
by Connie Donaldson

Connie Donaldson's technique for creating gorgeous butterflies and flower petals is brought to life on this lovely pendant of imitative stone.

Time Flies Clock
by Kim Cavender

Clocks have always been one of my favorite things to create with polymer clay. This one combines a textured Skinner blend sheet with a transfer technique and millefiori canework.

Starry Sky
Flower Pendant
by Donna Kato

This pendant by Donna Kato showcases her component caning technique that enables her to create beautiful painted effects using only polymer clay.

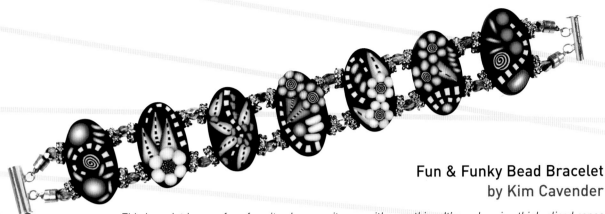

Fun & Funky Bead Bracelet
by Kim Cavender

This bracelet is one of my favorites because it goes with everything. It's made using thinly sliced canes applied to black base beads and strung with crystal and sterling beads and findings.

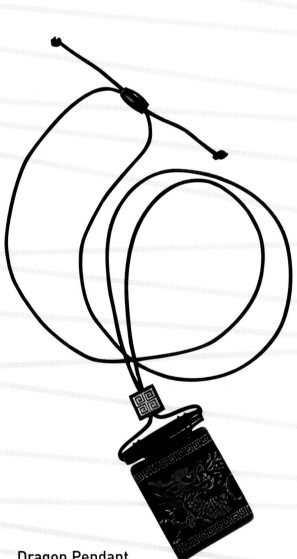

Dragon Pendant
by Jacqueline Lee

Jacqueline Lee has created an elegant pendant which has been carefully gilded with metallic powders. The dragon motif is striking against the black clay background.

Tessellations in Blue
Bracelet & Pendant
by Judy Belcher

This lovely bracelet and pendant set is created from slices of millefiori canes and further embellished with decorative borders. The beautiful finish was achieved through sanding and buffing.

123

RESOURCES

All of the supplies used to make the projects in this book can be found in your local craft, hobby, rubber stamping or discount department stores. If you have trouble locating a specific product, contact one of the manufacturers listed below to find a local vendor.

ALL THE WRITE NEWS
P.O. Box 67096, Los Angeles, CA 90067
(877) 877-2896
www.atwnstore.com
Pencil Grip craft knife

AMERICAN ART CLAY CO., INC. (AMACO)
6060 Guion Rd., Indianapolis, IN 46254
(800) 374-1600
www.amaco.com
wireform mesh, designer pushmolds, clay cutters

CLAY COMPANY
21136 S. Wilmington Ave., Carson, CA 90810
(866) 335-8333
www.claycompany.com
large leaf mold

CLEARSNAP
P.O. Box 98, Anacortes, WA 98221
(888) 448-4862
www.clearsnap.com
molding mats, MicaMagic stamp pads

CRAF-T PRODUCTS
P.O. Box 83
Fairmont, MN 56031
(507) 235-3996
www.craf-tproducts.com
decorating chalks

DECOART
P.O. Box 386, Stanford, KY 40484
(800) 367-3047
www.decoart.com
oak gel stain

DELTA TECHNICAL COATING INC.
2550 Pellisseir Pl., Whittier, CA 90601
(800) 423-4135
www.deltacrafts.com
Sobo glue, acrylic paint

EOFFICEDIRECT.COM
P.O. Box 1756, Bethlehem, PA 18016
(888) 363-8350
www.eofficedirect.com
letter opener, magnetic bookends

FIRE MOUNTAIN GEMS & BEADS
One Fire Mountain Way, Grants Pass, OR 97526
(800) 355-2137
www.firemountaingems.com
beads, jump rings, eye pins, head pins, earring findings, jewelry tools, Kato Polyclay

FISKARS
2537 Daniels St., Madison, WI 53718
(866) 348-5661
www.fiskars.com
texture plates, hand punches, rotary cutter and mat, hand drill

HEART IN HAND STUDIO/LISA PAVELKA
9825 Tarzana Ln., Las Vegas, NV 89117
(702) 765-5471
www.heartinhandstudio.com
rubber texture plates, Poly Bonder glue, sterling silver bezel setting, polymer clay foil, waterslide decals

HOUSTON ART, INC.
10770 Moss Ridge Rd.,
Houston, TX 77043
(800) 272-3804
www.houstonart.com
composition gold leaf

JUDIKINS
17803 S. Harvard Blvd., Gardena, CA 90248
(310) 515-1115
www.judikins.com
Metropolis background rubber stamp

KATO POLYCLAY/VAN AKEN INTERNATIONAL
P.O. Box 1680, Rancho Cucamonga, CA 91729
(909) 980-2001
www.katopolyclay.com
Kato Polyclay, clay blades, acrylic rollers, Marxit tool

KEMPER ENTERPRISES
13595 12th Street, Chino, CA 91710
(909) 627-6191
www.kempertools.com
Kemper pattern cutters, ball tip stylus, pro needle tool, clay blades, clay lift tool

KRAFTY LADY ART MOULDS
Rear 9 Edgewood Rd., Dandenong 3175, Victoria AU
(61) 3 9794 6064
www.kraftylady.com.au
mini torso mold

POLYMER CLAY EXPRESS (THE ARTWAY STORE)
9890 Main St., Damascus, MD 20872
(800) 844-0138
www.polymerclayexpress.com
buna cord, o-rings, polymer clay, tools and supplies

PRAIRIE CRAFT COMPANY
P.O. Box 209, Florissant, CO 80816
(800) 779-0615
www.prairiecraft.com
Kato Polyclay, Marxit, clay tools and accessories, books, videos

PRYM-DRITZ CORPORATION
P.O. Box 5028, Spartanburg, SC 29303
(864) 576-5050
www.dritz.com
Dritz Pop Top Carry Alls

RANGER INDUSTRIES, INC.
15 Park Road, Tinton Falls, NJ 07724
(732) 389-3535
www.rangerink.com
Adirondack alcohol inks, Perfect Pearls powders

RUPERT, GIBBON & SPIDER, INC.
(JACQUARD PRODUCTS)
P.O. Box 425, Healdsburg, CA 95448
(800) 442-0455
www.jacquardproducts.com
Piñata Colors (inks)

SCRATCH-ART CO., INC.
P.O. Box 303, Avon, MA 02322
(508) 583-8085
www.scratchart.com
Shade-Tex texture plates

STAMPENDOUS!
1240 N. Red Gum, Anaheim, CA 92806
(800) 869-0474
www.stampendous.com
Stitched Quill rubber stamp

THE STAMP BARN (STITTSVILLE RUBBER STAMP INC.)
1450 Stittsville Main St., Stittsville, ON Canada K2S 1A7
(800) 246-1142
www.stampbarn.com
alphabet tiles rubber stamp

TEESHA MOORE (ALTERNATIVE ARTS PRODUCTIONS)
Box 3329, Renton, WA 98056
www.teeshamoore.com
rubber stamps for clay notebook project

TONER PLASTICS
699 Silver St., Agawam, MA 01001
(413) 789-1300
www.tonerplastics.com
plastic-coated Fun Wire

TSUKINEKO, INC.
17640 N.E. 65th St., Redmond, WA 98052
(425) 883-7733
www.tsukineko.com
VersaCraft (Fabrico) craft ink pad, StazOn ink pad

VALKAT DESIGNS
P.O. Box 12563, Columbus, OH 43212
(614) 279-4790
Precise-a-Slice cane slicer

WALNUT HOLLOW
1409 SR 23, Dodgeville, WI 53533
(800) 950-5101
www.walnuthollow.com
wooden arch clock, clock movement, Makin's clay alphabet cutters

INDEX

Find more fun and creative inspiration and instruction in these fabulous North Light books

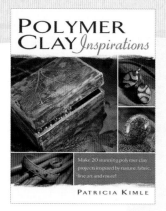

Polymer Clay Inspirations
by Patricia Kimle

Each of the beautiful projects featured in *Polymer Clay Inspirations* imitates nature, artwork, textiles and fine semi-precious stones in the elegant way that only the versatile medium of polymer clay can. You'll learn how to create fashionable wearable art, jewelry and home accessories. With the clear and simple step-by-step instructions, you'll surprise yourself with everything you'll be able to make—from a mother-of-pearl checkers set to a turquoise bracelet, there is no limit to what you can create with polymer clay.
ISBN 1-58180-557-8, paperback, 128 pages, 33013

Creative Techniques for Polymer Clay Jewelry
by Nanetta Bananto

Polymer clay jewelry has never been hotter, attracting a growing number of crafters eager to make beautiful jewelry with this exciting medium. The new polymer clay recruits join longtime enthusiasts who are always looking for fun, new projects. In this book, both groups get what they want. Inside, readers will find an extensive overview of polymer clay and jewelry-making basics as well as an extensive techniques section that instructs readers in making both simple and complex canes. Readers will love each of the 45 step-by-step projects, all of which include suggestions for variations so they can tailor the pieces to their personal tastes.
ISBN 1-58180-651-5, paperback, 128 pages, 33240

30-Minute Rubber Stamp Workshop
by Sandra McCall

Create a wonderful, personal gift in the time it takes to drive to the store! In *30-Minute Rubber Stamp Workshop*, Sandra McCall shows you how to handcraft gorgeous rubber stamped pieces without taking all day to do it. The time-saving tips and pre-chosen color combinations in the book will help you cut down on prep time and make projects fly out of your fingers. This must-have book features 30 quick and easy projects, including 11 wearable gifts such as pins, necklaces and bracelets. Through full-color illustrations and clear step-by-step instructions, you'll be making wonderful creations in no time.
ISBN 1-58180-271-4, paperback, 128 pages, 32142

Polymer Clay Extravaganza
by Lisa Pavelka

Fast and fun, this book features 20 dazzling projects that combine easy polymer clay techniques with a variety of accessible mediums, including mosaic, wire stamping, foiling, millefiore, caning and metal embossing. Step-by-step instructions, full-color photos and a section for beginners guarantees success. This unique guide also includes an inspiring idea gallery that encourages crafters to expand their creativity and develop original pieces of their own.
ISBN 1-58180-188-2, paperback, 128 pages, 31960

These and other fine North Light titles are available from
your local art and craft retailer, bookstore or online supplier.